A FALCON GUIDE®

D1499217

Exploring the Great Texas Coastal Birding Trail

Highlights of a Birding Mecca

Mel White

FALCON®

GUILFORD, CONNECTICUT
HELENA, MONTANA

AN IMPRINT OF THE GLOBE PEQUOT PRESS

Copyright © 2004 by The Globe Pequot Press

Text design by Nancy Freeborn
Photo courtesy Texas Parks & Wildlife © 2003, Earl Nottingham
Maps: XNR Productions Inc. © The Globe Pequot Press

Library of Congress Cataloging-in-Publication Data

White, Mel, 1950–
    Exploring the great Texas coastal birding trail : highlights of a birding Mecca / Mel White. — 1st ed.
        p. cm.
    Includes bibliographical references (p.) and index.
    ISBN 0-7627-2712-8
        1. Bird watching—Texas —Gulf Coast—Guidebooks. 2. Birding sites—Texas—Gulf Coast—Guidebooks. 3. Trails—Texas—Guidebooks. 4. Gulf Coast (Tex.)—Guidebooks. I. Title.

QL684.T4W485 2003
598'07'234764—dc22   2003056846

Manufactured in the United States of America
First Edition/First Printing

Contents

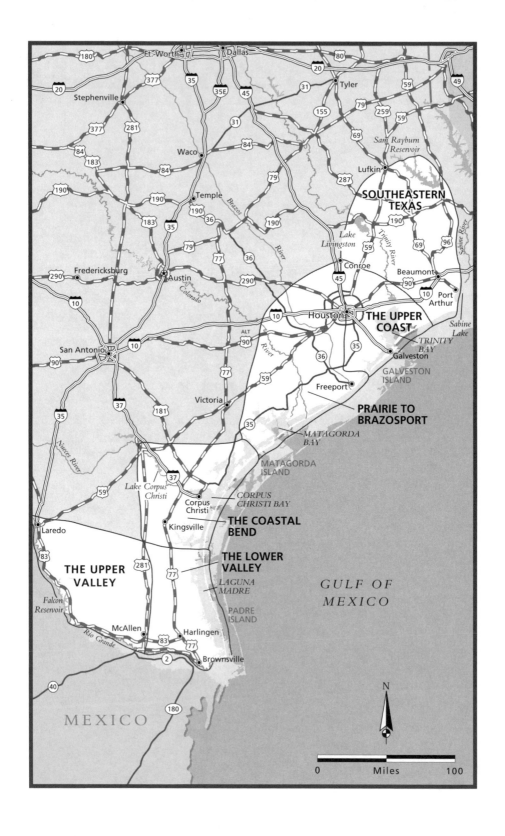

Texas: A Very Birdy Place

Birding is booming. The hobby (or, in many cases, passion, or even addiction) has been growing steadily for years, according to studies conducted by both governmental and private organizations. An amazing number of people—more than 70 million, by one 2001 survey of recreation preferences—say they participate in birdwatching.

Undoubtedly, many of these people simply put feeders in their backyards and enjoy watching the hummingbirds, chickadees, and goldfinches that show up. But just as certainly, more and more birders are venturing beyond their yards to discover the fun of seeing new birds in new places, whether it's a drive through a national wildlife refuge or a guided walk at a nature preserve.

Once someone has discovered the joys and challenges of birding—and perhaps subscribed to a birding magazine or attended meetings of a local bird club or Audubon chapter—it doesn't take long to learn that there are places in the United States that experienced birders visit as surely as geese fly south in the fall. These spots are to birders what the Rockies are to skiers or Pebble Beach is to golfers. Southeastern Arizona has its enthusiasts, as do southern Florida and southern California. And so, most assuredly, does the region encompassing the Texas Gulf Coast and the lower Rio Grande Valley. Visit one of the most popular sites here at the height of spring migration and you'll meet people not only from around the country but from around the world, so famous is the Texas coast as a birding destination.

One reason for this is diversity—a concept as important in birding as it is in so many other aspects of natural history. Eastern Texas marks the edge of the great sandy-soil pine forest of the southeastern United States as well as the limit of humid bottomland-hardwood forests reminiscent of the lower Mississippi River Alluvial Plain ("Delta"). Here and there are preserved remnant patches of the coastal tallgrass prairie that once stretched from Louisiana southwestward.

Moving down the coast, the land becomes more arid, the temperature hotter, the vegetation scrubbier, more like the American southwestern deserts.

Along the Rio Grande, remaining patches of thornscrub woodland and riparian forest create habitats unlike any other in the country. And all along the coast, of course, are saltwater and brackish marshes, beaches, bays protected by barrier islands, and the open waters of the Gulf of Mexico.

All these differing sorts of environments are, quite naturally, home to many more species of birds than would be found in forest, prairie, or marshland alone.

In addition to its varied habitats, the simple fact of its geographic location adds to the list of birds found along the Texas coast. Many migrant birds prefer to follow the coastline as they travel to and from Mexico and points south in fall and spring; as a result, they're funneled right through eastern Texas. One notable example is Broad-winged Hawk, a common migratory raptor of eastern American forests. In fall as they fly south, broadwings reach the Gulf Coast and follow it west and south. Literally hundreds of thousands of these birds pass along the coastline each year, only one of the most visible of scores of species that do the same.

Other birds fly northward in spring from Mexico straight across the Gulf of Mexico to the United States—quite a journey for small creatures with limited energy reserves. Many arrive at the Gulf Coast exhausted and hungry, and they drop out of the sky at the first land they see. Certain spots along the Texas coast have become world-famous for spring "fallouts" or "groundings" of migrant songbirds, when great numbers of species might be seen in a couple of hours in a single small woodlot. High Island, 55 miles east of Houston, is the most famous such site. In the fall migrant birds reach the coast and often stop in the same locations to rest and feed before continuing south.

Some birds normally found farther west in North America are seen along the Texas coast each year. Having strayed off their normal migration routes, these birds reach the Gulf of Mexico and simply stop, unwilling to continue their off-course journey. And there are seabirds, notorious for wandering long distances across their nearly featureless domain. Though not as rich in seabirds as, say, central California's coast, Texas gets its share of uncommon shearwaters, sea ducks, gulls, terns, and jaegers.

The Rio Grande forms Texas's southern border as well as the border between the United States and Mexico. The narrow stream is hardly an obstacle to birds, which need no passports to fly north to feed or nest in patches of preserved woodland along the river. Many "Mexican" species are found in the United States only in extreme southern Texas—a fact that has little biological significance but adds to the avian diversity of the state (and the nation) and provides yet another reason for U.S. birders to visit.

Given all this, it's no surprise that more than 450 species of birds have been seen along the Texas Gulf Coast and in the lower Rio Grande Valley. Some of these are once-in-a-decade rarities, but so rich is this region that many birders make regular visits year after year to enjoy a variety that, if not infinite, is at least infinitely fascinating.

The Great Texas Coastal Birding Trail: It Makes Sense

In 1988 a friend and I got off a jet at the Harlingen airport at the beginning of a birding trip to the Rio Grande Valley. We boarded a shuttle bus that would take us to our rental car, and the young man driving asked if we were heading over to South Padre Island for a beach vacation.

"We're down here to watch birds," I said. He turned to look at us with a puzzled expression.

"You know this is one of the most famous birdwatching spots around, don't you?" I asked. "You've got things that aren't found anywhere else in the country. Thousands of people come here every year to look for birds."

The driver said he had no idea. I was amazed. It was like living in Manhattan and not knowing that people visited to go to Broadway plays.

The driver's cluelessness was in a way understandable, though. Birders tend to sneak into a town, stay at inexpensive motels (why stay at a fancy place if you're never going to be there?), get up at dawn, eat on the run, spend the day in out-of-the-way parks and natural areas, and hit the sack early. Birders can be nearly invisible even in places that are (relatively speaking) thronged with them at certain times of the year.

To its credit, Texas woke up to the potential of birding tourism before most places. In the early 1990s, Texas birders and officials with the state Parks and Wildlife Department—encouraged by studies that showed birders contributing millions of dollars annually to some communities—began to consider a marked "trail" of highways and byways that would link favorite birding sites, making it easier for travelers to plan a trip and publicizing lesser-known destinations. And, of course, raising the profile of Texas coast birding in general.

This innovative route, christened the Great Texas Coastal Birding Trail, was completed in three stages. The central section was dedicated in 1995. In attendance was none other than Roger Tory Peterson, the creator of field guides that sparked the modern era of birdwatching and the person who symbolized the activity to millions of people. (Dr. Peterson died in 1996.) By April 2000 the upper and lower sections of the GTCBT were completed, linking more than 300 sites from the Piney Woods of eastern Texas to the Rio Grande Valley, a distance of more than 400 miles. The total number of sites was many more than the planners had originally envisioned; towns along the way, enthusiastic about the project, had nominated far more destinations than had been expected.

Other states and regions have noted the success of the GTCBT and have created, or begun to plan, similar birding routes. But Texas got there first—and even if other states imitate the concept, almost none can compete with Texas's birds.

Birding the Trail

The Texas Parks and Wildlife Department (TPWD) and the Department of Transportation offer three large maps corresponding to the upper, central, and lower sections of the GTCBT. Anyone planning a birding trip to the coast should order these maps, available by calling (888) TXBIRDS (892–4737), by searching on-line at www.tpwd.state.tx.us/birdingtrails/, or by writing Texas Parks and Wildlife Department, 4200 Smith School Road, Austin TX 78744. The maps are free, although a donation of $3.00 per map is requested; supporting the GTCBT is well worth the money. (Maps are also available at many tourist information centers, local tourist bureaus, and state parks.) For a general overview of the GTCBT, you can explore the Web site www.tpwd.state. tx.us/nature/ and its many links.

You might also consider ordering (for $2.00) *A Checklist of Texas Birds*, a brochure that lists all the species found in the state and has boxes for recording sightings, making it a convenient way to keep up with what you see on a birding trip. Write to the previous TPWD address.

One side of each GTCBT map is a somewhat stylized regional map indicating site locations. The other side identifies sites by number (e.g., UTC 15 is Upper Texas Coast site number 15, Big Thicket National Preserve), gives brief directions and descriptions, and lists notable birds and tips for finding them. The sites are arranged by color-coded "loops" (suggested driving routes grouping proximate locations), which sometimes means that sites near each other geographically are not listed together on the map.

The GTCBT's more than 300 sites range from national wildlife refuges with tens of thousands of acres, well-marked auto-tour routes, and all sorts of available maps and brochures to small city parks to simply stretches of isolated road passing through birdy habitat. Brown highway signs marked with the profile of a Black Skimmer identify locations by number. Most sites are free to enter; some (including state parks) charge admission; some are on private property where entry is in some way limited to those with prior permission or to paying guests.

On the upper coast, spring is the essential time for a birding trip, especially a first visit. Songbirds are in their brightest plumage, and many are singing, making them easier to find. Not only are the resident birds present, but migrants passing through on their way north swell each day's list. Interesting breeding birds are around in summer, but as the season progresses they sing less, and conditions get hotter and buggier.

Many local birders on the upper coast spend as much time in the field in fall as in spring; though the famous migrant-bird locations aren't as productive in the number of individual birds seen, rarities often show up at this time of year. After nesting, some species (especially young birds) have a tendency to wander far from their normal ranges. Fall brings waves of migrant shorebirds, with their attendant challenges to identification, and makes a visit to any beach or mudflat a potentially rewarding experience.

Spring is of course a great time to bird the central coast and the Rio Grande Valley, too. The farther south you go, the hotter the summer gets. Midsummer in the Valley can be almost unbearable soon after sunrise. But if that's the only time you can visit this fabulous destination, you'll still be able to see its special nesting birds.

Winter can be a great time anywhere along the coast. Huge flocks of waterfowl can be seen in many places, and the beaches are dotted with waders and shorebirds. Whooping Cranes, perhaps the most famous endangered species on the coast, are present in and near Aransas National Wildlife Refuge; they attract hundreds of birders eager to see this legendary creature. Winter is a favorite time for many birders to visit the Rio Grande Valley—a warm haven from snow and chill up north. There are experienced birders who visit the Valley each winter the way football fanatics make plans to attend each year's Super Bowl.

Logistically speaking, the Texas Gulf Coast is an easy place to bird. With the exception of Houston, and to a lesser degree Corpus Christi, there are no large cities to deal with and few traffic-choked freeways. The Texas state highway system is excellent. What may on the map appear to be minor roads are often wide, well-paved and well-marked highways. Those looking for vast wilderness areas and untouched spaces won't find them here—but the positive side is the fact that towns with motels, restaurants, and other amenities are usually nearby, wherever you go.

On the good news/bad news subject as well: The topography that makes this area so easy to travel in also means you won't find much picturesque scenery. The Texas Gulf Coast is composed of some of the youngest land in North America. For sixty million years, the Gulf of Mexico has been retreating, while the land, freed of the weight of the sea, has risen. At the same time, rivers such as the Sabine, the Trinity, the Brazos, and the Colorado have been carrying gravel, sand, and silt from the plains and spreading the material along the shore. The Mississippi, too, has contributed to building Texas; the silt it carries to the gulf in such massive quantity is carried west by currents and deposited along the coastline—or at least it was, until humans began interfering with the river's natural delta formation.

Its alluvial creation, with its raw material constantly washed and sorted by rivers and tides, means the Texas coast is flat. Bluffs punctuate the coast near Corpus Christi, but in many places the roof of an RV is the high point in the general vicinity. Up in the Piney Woods north of Houston, ancient dunes and other beach deposits created sandstone hills, but those are rolling rather than lofty. The town of Alto got its name because it was a "high" point along the

Old Spanish Trail trade route, but its elevation is only 433 feet. While there are pretty microenvironments—a nicely wooded trail, or a lonely beach—often the best scenery around is a Scarlet Tanager or a Green Jay.

The hazards of a Texas coastal birding trip are few. Hurricanes or tropical storms can strike the coast in late summer and fall, but weather forecasts give ample warning. Winter weather is very rarely a problem anywhere.

Alligators are present at some birding destinations; a little caution (maintaining a safe distance and never, ever feeding them) removes nearly all the danger. Most birders are thrilled, rather than frightened, by the chance to see gators. Poisonous snakes are a somewhat greater risk; cottonmouths (water moccasins) are common in some swampy and marshy spots, and various species of rattlesnakes are found in a variety of habitats. Watching where you put your feet and hands and not walking out into grassy spots where you can't see where you're stepping are the standard rules for avoiding snakes.

For most people, the nastiest animal along the Texas coast is the mosquito. At times, in humid locations, this insect can be present in such numbers that birding is nearly impossible. And that's the case even when you've taken the usual steps of wearing long pants and long sleeves and using repellent. In such circumstances, the only choice may be a quick retreat. Often a patch of woods may be swarming with mosquitoes, while an open area nearby may be windy enough to keep them at bay. In other words, forget the warblers and enjoy the wading birds and sparrows.

Some Addresses and Numbers

To order a comprehensive (and free) travel guide to Texas, go on-line to www.traveltex.com, or call (800) 452–9292; you can also get the official state highway map and an accommodations guide. In the travel guide and on the Web site you'll find the addresses, phone numbers, and, often, Web sites of city and regional tourist bureaus throughout the state.

For information on Texas state parks, call (800) 792–1112 or visit www.tpwd.state.tx.us on the Internet. Note that to make camping reservations for state parks, you must call a different number: (512) 389–8900.

If you plan on an extensive trip along the coast, visiting many state parks, it can be cost-effective to buy a $50 Texas Conservation Passport, which allows free entrance to all state parks and wildlife management areas (WMAs) for you and the passengers in your vehicle. The passport is good for one year from the date of purchase. You can buy a passport at any state park. For information, call (800) 792–1112 or go to www.tpwd.state.tx.us on the Internet.

To visit most state wildlife management areas, you must have either a Conservation Passport, a Texas state hunting license, or a Limited Use Permit

($10), the last of which is available from TPWD or wherever hunting licenses are sold. At this writing, however, the issue of fees for birders visiting WMAs was still being debated. For example, no permit is required to visit the hawk-watch tower at "Candy" Abshier WMA (UTC 48) or to walk the nature trail at the Longoria Unit of Las Palomas WMA (LTC16). For the latest requirements, contact TPWD.

Before traveling, experienced birders know to check the rare-bird alerts (RBAs) for the areas they'll be visiting. These alerts are recorded messages, maintained by local bird groups, listing significant sightings. Calling an RBA can let you know that, for example, Swallow-tailed Kites have been appearing at a spot near Houston, or a Yellow-faced Grassquit has been hanging around in the Rio Grande Valley. These numbers tend to change occasionally, but current numbers are:

- Texas statewide: (713) 369–9673
- Rio Grande Valley: (956) 584–2731

The Internet has, of course, changed the process of doing research for a birding trip. A couple of hours searching and browsing can save time, find current information, and turn up all sorts of helpful advice, including names of local birders willing to help visitors. We won't attempt to list many Web sites here, since they change often. However, the www.traveltex.com site has a "Birding" section with links to a great number of parks, refuges, cities, and organizations. Check also www.tpwd.state.tx.us/nature/birding, which has general advice and a list of Texas Audubon groups and other bird clubs, with links to Web sites and local contact names.

Nature Festivals

A good way for a newcomer to get acquainted with the birds of a region is at a birding or nature festival. Increasingly, cities are organizing and promoting these celebrations as a way to attract visitors, raise the profile of their area as a destination, and, of course, make money for local businesses. In the process residents and politicians—whether nature lovers or not—may come to realize that their parks, preserves, and other natural areas have financial as well as environmental value, and so support their protection.

Festivals can include programs (sometimes with local naturalists, often with national experts), exhibits, and field trips. Sometimes these trips visit areas not regularly accessible by the public. In addition to offering a chance to see special birds, attending a festival can simply be a lot of fun, encouraging the camaraderie that many birders find one of the main attractions of the pursuit.

Many of the nature festivals of the GTCBT region will be discussed in the main body of the book, in the appropriate geographical area. Here is a quick listing, arranged by dates:

- Port Aransas: A Celebration of Whooping Cranes & Other Birds, February, (800) 452–6278. www.portaransas.org
- McAllen: Texas Tropics Nature Festival, March, (877) 622–5536; www.mcallenchamber.com
- Kountze: Birding In The Big Thicket, April, (866) 456–8689; www.kountzecoc.org
- Galveston: FeatherFest, April, (888) 425–4753; www.galvestonfeatherfest.com
- Eagle Lake: Attwater's Prairie Chicken Festival, April, (979) 234–3021 or (979) 234–2780; www.visiteaglelake.com
- Lake Jackson: Migration Celebration, May, (800) 938–4853 or (979) 480–0999; refugefriends.org
- Brownsville: Brownsville International Birding Festival, July, (800) 626–2639; www.brownsville.org
- Lake Jackson: Xtreme Hummingbird Xtravaganza, September, (979) 480–0999; www.gcbo.org
- Rockport: Hummer/Bird Celebration, September, (800) 826–6441; www.rockport-fulton.org
- Corpus Christi: A Celebration of Flight, September, (361) 241–2920; www.electrotex.com/AOC
- Raymondville: Wild in Willacy, October, (888) 603–6994; www.wildinwillacy.com
- Kingsville: South Texas Wildlife and Birding Festival, November, (361) 592–8516; www.kingsvilletexas.com
- Harlingen: Rio Grande Valley Birding Festival, November, (800) 531–7346; www.rgvbirdfest.com

How This Book Is Arranged

Practical reasons of space prevent us from covering in detail all 300-plus sites of the Great Texas Coastal Birding Trail. (And, in fact, even some supporters of the trail admit that some sites were selected because of political pressure or tourism promotion rather than because of their birding quality.) We have selected about one hundred of the best locations along the trail, chosen for diversity (of habitat, species, and seasonality), productivity, and accessibility. The sites in this book are identified with their official GTCBT numbers (e.g., CTC 37, or Central Texas Coast site 37)—the same numbers found on the GTCBT maps. In some cases the names of sites in the book may not match those on the maps because of changes made since the maps were printed.

In this book the sites are divided into six chapters, beginning in the eastern Texas Piney Woods, continuing south along the Gulf Coast to the Rio Grande (the U.S.-Mexican border), and then moving upriver about 180 miles. Sometimes sites are covered individually; sometimes proximate sites are grouped under one heading. The order of sites in this book does not correspond to the order on the GTCBT maps, which—because they combine locations into driving "loops" in three geographic regions—sometimes give nearby sites unrelated numbers. (This book isn't immune to that somewhat unavoidable situation, either. For example, note that the W. Goodrich Jones State Forest, in the Southeastern Texas chapter, is fairly close to the Katy Prairie, in the Prairie to Brazosport chapter.)

The site listings give general, and often specific, directions (we assume you have an official state highway map), contact information (including Web sites when available), advice about when and how to bird the location, and a listing of some of the notable species that might be found. When a site requires an admission fee, that fact is noted.

We also discuss some non-GTCBT attractions along the way, including museums and nature centers, that travelers may find worthwhile. These attractions range from the Museum of Natural Science in downtown Houston to the Gladys Porter Zoo in Brownsville.

More and more bed-and-breakfast inns are opening that especially cater to birders. We list a number of these inns, with brief descriptions—and with the caveat that such establishments tend to open and close and change ownership frequently. While the list is accurate as of the time of printing, a request for information before booking is always worthwhile.

We list a few of the nature festivals held annually along the GTCBT as well, with details about their general themes and activities. They, too, evolve over time, so a request for information well ahead of time is vital before planning a trip around one. Check the Web site www.birdwatchersdigest.com/festivals/festivals.html for sources of current information about nature festivals.

Acknowledgments

Among those who offered help and information were John C. Arvin, Chris Battan, Steve Benn, Kathy Adams Clark, Fred Collins, Mel Cooksey, Larry Ditto, Martin Hagne, Petra Hockey, David Lee, Richard Lehman, Brad McKinney, Ken Merritt, Nancy Millar, Ann Neese, Jimmy Paz, John Ross, Don Verser, Jerry Walls, Ron Weeks, and Jennifer Wilson. None of these people, of course, is responsible for any errors in the book.

Southeastern Texas

Eastern Texas is the anomaly of the Great Texas Coastal Birding Trail. Instead of sandy shore, brackish marshes, and flat, scrubby woodland, here you'll find beautiful forests, meandering rivers, and rolling hills. Instead of beach, beech.

In this region you'll explore the western limit of the great forest of longleaf, shortleaf, and loblolly pines that stretches across the Southeast to the Atlantic coast. Texans call it their part of it the Piney Woods, and though it's been heavily exploited for timber, it still contains places of great scenic and ecological value. Four national forests cover more than 1,000 square miles of eastern Texas, and in many areas active management programs are attempting to restore the fire-maintained ecosystem of open woods and grassy understory that the first European settlers encountered. Many miles of trails and several wilderness areas invite those who seek solitude.

Here, too, are hardwood forests of oak, beech, magnolia, sweet gum, and holly, as well as bottomland swamps with bald cypress and tupelo, more reminiscent of Mississippi than of Texas. A sampling of this diversity lies within Big Thicket National Preserve, protected by the National Park Service after decades of struggle between conservationists and timber and oil companies.

Birders visit eastern Texas to look for Swallow-tailed Kite; Red-cockaded Woodpecker; Brown-headed Nuthatch; Worm-eating, Swainson's, and Hooded warblers; and Bachman's Sparrow, among other species. It would be a shame, though, to dart single-mindedly from one birding site to another and not take time to enjoy a hike in spots such as Big Creek Scenic Area, in the Sam Houston National Forest east of Conroe.

This chapter also touches on the Gulf Coast, where flocks of wading birds and shorebirds create the kind of spectacle that many people think of when they think of the GTCBT, and where songbirds can drop from the sky in colorful multitudes in spring "fallouts." But more on that in the next chapter.

As you plan your travels in this region, note that Texas Highway 87 is closed from High Island east to near Sea Rim State Park, which translates to a looping route through Winnie as you travel between the extreme eastern Gulf Coast and birding sites nearer Galveston.

Southeastern Texas

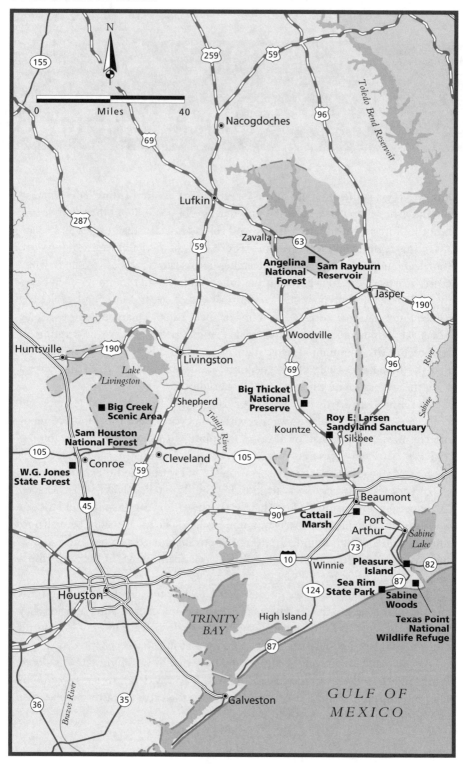

N

155

0   Miles   40

259   59

Nacogdoches

96

Toledo Bend Reservoir

69

Lufkin

287

Zavalla   63

59

Angelina
National
Forest

Sam Rayburn
Reservoir

Jasper   190

Woodville

Huntsville   190

Livingston

69

96

Lake
Livingston

Sabine River

Shepherd

Big Thicket
National
Preserve

Big Creek
Scenic Area

Trinity River

Kountze

Roy E. Larsen
Sandyland Sanctuary

Sam Houston
National Forest

Silsbee

105   Cleveland   105

59

W.G. Jones
State Forest

Conroe

Beaumont

45

90   Cattail
Marsh

Port
Arthur

Sabine
Lake

10   Winnie

73

Pleasure
Island

82

124   Sea Rim
State Park

87

Sabine
Woods

Houston

TRINITY
BAY

High Island

Texas Point
National
Wildlife Refuge

87

Brazos River

36   35

Galveston

GULF OF
MEXICO

Angelina National Forest

Vast parklike areas of longleaf pine once grew in the part of eastern Texas called the Piney Woods, but after decades of logging very little of this natural environment remains. The huge pines, which had stood for centuries, were just too valuable to survive once the American frontier moved west and timber companies moved in.

Four national forests—Sabine, Angelina, Sam Houston, and Davy Crockett—cover more than 660,000 acres of pine-hardwood forest in this region today. Like many national forests, they serve in large part as tree farms for timber and pulpwood. Here and there, though, designated areas are managed to protect and restore longleaf habitat and to benefit endangered species.

When birders think of southeastern pine forests, they often think of the Red-cockaded Woodpecker (RCW). This endangered species requires mature pine woods with an open understory; timber cutting and fire suppression have eliminated it or reduced its population over most of its range. In several national forests, however, RCWs are holding their own or increasing, thanks to management programs (including controlled burning) that encourage the kind of woodland the species needs. Another bird benefiting from such programs is Bachman's Sparrow (once called Pinewoods Sparrow), often found nesting in the same open, grassy pine habitat as RCWs.

In the southern part of the Angelina National Forest, southeast of the town of Zavalla, you'll find a pleasant area to camp, hike, swim, and look for typical Piney Woods birds. Nearby, the sprawling Sam Rayburn Reservoir offers the chance to look for wintering loons, grebes, Bald Eagles, and waterfowl.

From the intersection of U.S. Highway 69 and Texas Highway 63 in Zavalla, drive southeast on TX 63 for 11 miles to Forest Road 313 (Boykin Springs Road) and turn south. In 1.4 miles you'll see an area of excellent longleaf pinewoods on the west; some trees here are well over one hundred years old. Red-cockaded Woodpecker and Bachman's Sparrow (spring and summer) are here, as is Brown-headed Nuthatch, another pinewoods specialist. You may also see typical eastern Texas species such as Great Crested Flycatcher; White-eyed and Yellow-throated vireos; Pine Warbler; Yellow-breasted Chat; and Painted Bunting. Henslow's Sparrow has been found in wet, grassy spots in winter. Botanists know this area as home to many rare or unusual plants, including ferns, orchids, and insect-eating sundews and pitcher plants.

Continue another mile to the Boykin Springs Recreation Area (UTC 7; fee), a popular Angelina National Forest site with camping and swimming at a small, spring-fed lake. From here, the Sawmill Hiking Trail runs 5.5 miles to Bouton Lake (UTC 8), another national forest site with primitive camping and a small lake. (Bouton Lake is reached by car by turning south on Forest Road 303 from TX 63, 7 miles southeast of Zavalla.)

From Boykin Springs, the Sawmill Trail runs alongside Boykin Creek for a mile or so through pretty, rolling woodland. It then meets the Neches River, following its north bank along sandy bluffs to Bouton Lake. Although there are no especially notable birds here, this is a fine walk through a forest of loblolly pine, bald cypress, river birch, water and swamp chestnut oaks, American holly, and sweet gum. Look for (among many others) Great Blue Heron; Wood Duck; Red-shouldered Hawk; Belted Kingfisher; Pileated Woodpecker; Acadian Flycatcher; Northern Parula; Prothonotary and Hooded warblers; and Louisiana Waterthrush.

From fall to spring while you're in this area, it can be worthwhile to check Sam Rayburn Reservoir (UTC 6). To reach it from Boykin Springs, return to TX 63 and drive 7 miles southeast; turn northeast on Texas Highway 255R and drive 6 miles to the massive dam. At the Corps of Engineers office here, you can pick up a map showing recreation areas along shoreline of this huge body of water. Ebenezer, Overlook, and Twin Dikes parks are all found adjacent to the dam, and from each you can scan the lake for wintering Common Loon, grebes, ducks, and for an occasional Bald Eagle. An Osprey might show up in spring or fall migration.

National Forests in Texas
Homer Garrison Federal Building
701 North First Street
Lufkin, TX 75901
(936) 639–8501
www.southernregion.fs.fed.us/texas

Sam Rayburn Reservoir
Route 3, Box 486
Jasper, TX 75951
(409) 384–5716
www1.swf-wc.usace.army.mil/samray/

Big Creek Scenic Area

For a chance to see many of the typical birds of the eastern Texas Piney Woods/Big Thicket region, you could hardly do better than to take a short (or longer) hike along the trails at this beautiful spot located just a few minutes off U.S. Highway 59. A specially designated area within the Sam Houston National Forest, Big Creek encompasses 1,460 acres of meandering creeks, lush pine-hardwood forest, and varied flora and fauna.

From Shepherd take Texas Highway 150 west about 5 miles and turn southwest on Forest Road 217. In 2 miles you'll reach the parking area for the Big Creek trailhead. Once you're in the woods, you can choose from a series of color-coded, intersecting loops. The Pine Trail is 0.75 mile; the White Oak Trail is 1.5 miles; the Big Creek Trail is 2 miles, with the 0.5-mile Magnolia Trail as an optional addition. All connect with the Lone Star Hiking Trail, a 140-mile backpacking route that runs the whole length of the national forest. (The Lone Star leads 3 miles north to the Double Lake national forest recreation area, where you can find campsites and swimming.)

Whichever route you take, you'll see loblolly pine; American beech; black tupelo; white, swamp chestnut, water, and willow oaks; sweet gum, American hornbeam; southern and sweet bay magnolias; sassafras, yaupon, red bay, arrowwood, and palmetto. The Big Creek area has been protected since the 1960s, and many of the trees are impressively tall.

Nesting birds you may see or hear include Red-shouldered Hawk; Barred Owl; Yellow-billed Cuckoo; Pileated Woodpecker; Eastern Wood-Pewee; Acadian and Great Crested flycatchers; White-eyed, Yellow-throated, and Red-eyed vireos; Wood Thrush; Pine, Black-and-white, Worm-eating, Kentucky, and Hooded warblers; Louisiana Waterthrush; and Summer Tanager.

Although migrant songbirds aren't as concentrated in these extensive pinewood forests as they are in small coastal woodlots, Big Creek is certainly a wonderful place to be on a spring morning, when breeding birds are supplemented by transients and the area can be alive with the songs of dozens of species.

Be aware that Big Creek and its smaller tributaries can flood parts of the area at times, so certain sections of trail may be swampy or even under water.

For a chance to see the endangered Red-cockaded Woodpecker (RCW), which lives exclusively in open, mature pinewoods, continue southwest on FR 217 a little more than a mile to its intersection with paved Texas Highway 2666. Drive west on TX 2666 for 2 miles to Texas Highway 2025. Turn south and drive a short distance to a roadside interpretive area where the small, black-and-white woodpeckers nest. Early morning and late afternoon are the best times to see RCWs, when the birds leave their roost trees to forage and return for the evening.

There's another designated viewing area for RCWs farther west in the Sam Houston National Forest, very convenient for those traveling on I–45. From the interstate at New Waverly, take Texas Highway 1375 west 4.5 miles to a parking area on the south side of the highway.

National Forests in Texas
Homer Garrison Federal Building
701 North First Street
Lufkin, TX 75901
(936) 639–8501
www.southernregion.fs.fed.us/texas

A B&B for Birders

Christmas Creek Nature Preserve

Set on thirteen acres surrounded by the pinelands of the Sam Houston National Forest about 20 miles southwest of Huntsville (off Texas Highway 149, 1 mile west of its intersection with Texas Highway 1791), this bed-and-breakfast facility was completed in 2003. It comprises two rooms, one a separate cabin and the other in the lodge where the owners live. Operated by a local birding guide, the B&B was designed especially for birders and other nature enthusiasts. A trail winds through the property alongside Christmas Creek, and feeders and plantings attract birds and butterflies. Two groups of endangered Red-cockaded Woodpeckers are located nearby, and the national forest's Little Lake Wilderness Area is less than a mile away. Customized birding tours can be arranged by advance reservation.

Christmas Creek Nature Preserve
20841 Welch Road
Richards, TX 77873
(936) 857–0114
www.christmascreek.com

W. Goodrich Jones State Forest

The 1,745-acre Jones State Forest has long been known as one of the easiest sites in Texas at which to find the endangered Red-cockaded Woodpecker (RCW). The small black-and-white bird is a specialist of mature pinewoods, and Jones, established in 1926, encompasses areas of loblolly and shortleaf pine ranging from sixty to one hundred years old.

In 2003 there were fifteen clusters, or small family groups, of RCWs on the forest. One cluster was located adjacent to the forest office on Texas Highway 1488, just 1.5 miles west of I–45, southwest of Conroe. Another cluster was less than a quarter mile northwest, and the birds were often seen foraging in the pines around the office. Early morning and late afternoon are best for finding RCWs, and knowing their raspy call is very helpful.

Try to visit Jones on a weekday if you can, when the office is open. The staff welcomes visitors, and personnel are happy to provide maps and a bird list and to provide directions and advice for seeing RCWs.

Jones is a demonstration forest for researching management techniques and is not oriented toward recreation. Most of the roads are gated much of the time, but birders may walk in along any of the roads at any time. Parking is available at the office on TX 1488; at the end of Cochran Road, leading off TX 1488 south of the office; and at Jones Park, south of TX 1488, 0.8 mile west of the office. Two RCW clusters are located along Gravel Pit Road, which leads between the last two parking areas mentioned.

Brown-headed Nuthatch, another southern pine specialist, is common year-round at Jones, but Bachman's Sparrow—often found in pines with the nuthatch and RCWs—is uncommon to rare in spring and summer (look in open, grassy areas).

Oaks, hickories, magnolias, black gum, maples, and many other hardwoods are common in the forest, and there are scattered wetlands, all of which provide habitat for nesting birds including Wood Duck; Red-shouldered and Broad-winged hawks; Northern Bobwhite; American Woodcock; Barred Owl; White-eyed and Yellow-throated vireos; Wood Thrush; Northern Parula; and Yellow-throated, Pine, Prothonotary, Worm-eating, and Hooded warblers. Swainson's Warbler is an uncommon but regular breeder in areas of palmetto slough, such as those in the southeast and extreme northeast (north of TX 1488) parts of the forest.

Rapidly becoming surrounded by the burgeoning suburbs of Houston, Jones State Forest increases in importance as a natural area year by year—not just for the endangered Red-cockaded Woodpecker but for all the animals and plants that find a refuge here from strip malls and subdivisions.

W. Goodrich Jones State Forest
1328 FM 1488
Conroe, TX 77384
(936) 273–2261
txforestservice.tamu.edu

Big Thicket National Preserve and Roy E. Larsen Sandyland Sanctuary

Big Thicket National Preserve was established as a unit of the National Park Service in 1974, the result of a long and controversial struggle between conservationists, who wanted to save one of Texas's richest and most diverse ecosystems, and representatives of timber and oil companies, who fought the park with money and political influence. It now consists of several disjunct land areas, plus protected stretches of the Neches River and other waterways. The preserve totals almost 100,000 acres—only a fraction of the densely forested region that settlers nicknamed the Big Thicket. It's called a preserve rather than a national park because hunting and oil and gas exploration are allowed within its boundaries.

Botanists know the Big Thicket as home to twenty kinds of orchids, four kinds of carnivorous plants, and an array of other species reflecting a blend of southern bottomland woods (including the specialized wetland called baygall), pine savanna, and drier southwestern habitat. Birders know it as a place where trails, roads, and streams provide access to diverse environments and an equally varied set of birds.

The preserve's visitor center is located north of Kountze, at the intersection of Texas Highway 420 and US 69/287. Inside you'll find a video presentation on Big Thicket history (both human and natural), interactive displays, exhibits on flora and fauna, and activities for children.

Drive east 2.6 miles on TX 420 to the trailhead for one of the preserve's nicest walks. The Kirby Nature Trail, beginning near the former preserve visitor information station, encompasses a series of loops offering options from

1.7 to 5 miles. Loblolly pines, bald cypresses, beeches, magnolias, oaks, and sweet gums tower over swampy wetlands. A few of the birds you'll find here in spring and summer are Red-shouldered Hawk; Barred Owl; Pileated Woodpecker; Acadian and Great Crested flycatchers; Yellow-throated and Red-eyed vireos; Wood Thrush; Prothonotary, Yellow-throated, and Hooded warblers; Northern Parula; Louisiana Waterthrush; and Summer Tanager. With some luck (knowing its forceful, whistled song helps) you could find a Swainson's Warbler, a somewhat shy bird of canebrakes and thickets. The Sandhill Loop adjoins the Kirby Trail, passing through a drier habitat with longleaf pines. Here you could find Brown-headed Nuthatch, Pine and Prairie warblers, and Bachman's Sparrow, the last a sweet-singing specialist of open pinewoods.

While you're in this area, the preserve's Turkey Creek Unit, travel north to walk at least a portion of the Turkey Creek and Pitcher Plant trails, the latter a spectacular sight in spring with its insect-eating yellow pitcher plants and sweet bay magnolias. The lovely rose pogonia orchid is often seen along the Pitcher Plant Trail as well. Swainson's Warbler can be found in the Turkey Creek Trail's baygalls: wetlands dominated by sweet bay magnolia, gallberry holly, titi, red bay, and other swamp-loving species.

To the east, the preserve's Neches Bottom and Jack Gore Baygall Unit provides access to the Neches River bottomland, where among the many birds you might see are Anhinga; Green Heron; Yellow-crowned Night-Heron; Wood Duck; and Red-shouldered Hawk. Timber Slough Road, running east from Texas Highway 2937, leads to one typical area of wet woods dominated by bald cypress and water tupelo.

As usual, finding the greatest number of birds in the Big Thicket results from visiting a number of different habitats. Be sure to walk the short, easy Sundew Trail, in the Hickory Creek Savannah Unit (just west of US 69/287), where pine savanna offers another chance to see Brown-headed Nuthatch and Bachman's Sparrow, as well as the small, easily overlooked carnivorous plants for which the trail is named. Farther west, off Texas Highway 1276, the Woodlands Trail in the Big Sandy Creek Unit passes through beautiful mature hardwood forest as well as areas of scrubby second growth, where trees are regrowing in old pasture. Look here for species such as White-eyed Vireo, Prairie Warbler, and Painted Bunting.

Good roads make it easy to visit several units of Big Thicket National Preserve in a day. It can be a great birding experience, but take time, too, to learn about the diverse habitats and fascinating array of plants that make this one of the most important ecosystems in Texas.

While you're in the Big Thicket area, visit the Nature Conservancy's Roy E. Larsen Sandyland Sanctuary (UTC 17), a 5,651-acre tract located on Texas Highway 327 west of Silsbee. Village Creek winds through the area for 8 miles, lined by bald cypress and water tupelo. Local outfitters offer canoe trips along this very pretty stream, making for a leisurely birding day. Six miles of trails and old roads allow hiking through the sanctuary, which encompasses some of the same environments as the national preserve but includes areas of drier, sandy-soil habitat with longleaf pine, bluejack oak, yucca, and prickly pear. The bird list here is not as extensive as that of the national preserve, but a walk along the quiet trails will give you another chance to spot Red-shouldered Hawk; Greater Roadrunner; Barred Owl; Fish Crow; Brown-headed Nuthatch; and Pine Warbler year-round, and, in spring and summer, Yellow-crowned Night-Heron and Yellow-throated and Prothonotary warblers.

Big Thicket National Preserve
3785 Milam Street
Beaumont, TX 77701
(409) 246–2337
www.nps.gov/bith

Roy E. Larsen Sandyland Sanctuary
Nature Conservancy of Texas
P.O. Box 909
Silsbee, TX 77656
(409) 385–0445
www.texasnature.org/profiles/sandy.htm

Pelt Farm

The owners of a longtime family farm in the Big Thicket woods have remodeled an 1840s log dogtrot house to create a two-room bed-and-breakfast inn. Both rooms (themed Lone Star and French Country) have private baths and look out on landscaped grounds filled with live oaks, antique rose varieties, and azaleas, as well as butterfly gardens. Unusual varieties of domestic animals roam the grounds, and the innkeepers also display a collection of folk art and artifacts from the Piney Woods region. Pelt Farm is located off Texas Highway 421, about 1.4 miles east of Texas Highway 326, near the Lance Rosier Unit of Big Thicket National Preserve (UTC 15) and about 22 miles from the preserve visitor center.

> Pelt Farm
> 12487 Pelt Road
> Kountze, TX 77625
> (409) 287–3300
> www.peltfarm.com

Cattail Marsh

Excellent concentrations of wading birds, waterfowl, and shorebirds can be seen at this wetlands complex in Beaumont, located less than five minutes from I–10. To reach it, from I–10 south of its intersection with US 69/96/287, take the Walden Road exit, and drive south half a mile to Texas Highway 124. Continue south on Tyrrell Park Road and in 0.7 mile turn left into Tyrrell Park. Follow the main park road past the golf course and stables, around the picnic-area loop to the entry to Cattail Marsh.

The large ponds here were built as part of the Beaumont wastewater-treatment facility, and have created wetlands attractive to a variety of waterbirds. The complex is located adjacent to Hillebrandt and Willow Marsh bayous, which makes the area even more bird-friendly. To look for birds you must walk the levees between the ponds, which cover an area of more than a square mile. A spotting scope is very helpful.

In recent years a resident colony of waders has included Great, Snowy, and Cattle (most common) egrets; Little Blue, Tricolored, and Green herons; Black-crowned and Yellow-crowned night-herons; and White and White-faced ibises. Among other species often present seasonally are Pied-billed Grebe (Least, Horned, and Eared have all been seen); American White Pelican; Double-crested and Neotropic cormorants; Anhinga; Roseate Spoonbill; Fulvous and Black-bellied whistling-ducks; Wood and Mottled ducks; and Red-shouldered Hawk. In winter, many species of ducks can always be found resting and feeding here.

Shorebirds can be common in spring, late summer, and fall, though their presence depends on water levels in ponds creating the proper combinations of shallow water and mudflats. Marsh Wren is often present in the wetland vegetation, and Northern Harrier searches winter ponds for prey. Also in winter, Orange-crowned Warbler and White-crowned Sparrow can be found in the shrubby vegetation along the levees.

It requires a bit of walking to check out the ponds. There are about 8 miles of levees here and little shade, so bring water if you plan extensive exploration. (Some local birders ride their bikes to cover the area.)

Tyrrell Park is known as a place to see Fish Crow, a species not easy to find in this part of the state. Fish Crow looks exactly like American Crow and must be distinguished by its nasal, two-note call.

Cattail Marsh
P.O. Box 3827
Beaumont, TX 77704
(409) 866–0023
www.cattailmarsh.org

Pleasure Island

This partly artificially created "island" comprises a long strip of land separating the Intracoastal Waterway from Sabine Lake (the broad body of water just north of the Sabine River's mouth at the Gulf of Mexico). Just minutes from Port Arthur, it's home to recreation areas, a marina, restaurants, and condominiums. Birders visit it to drive its long levees in search of waterbirds. Pleasure Island is easy to bird from your vehicle, and it's worth a visit from fall through spring. It's only a few minutes out of the way for those heading south on TX 87 toward Sabine Woods (UTC 26) and Sea Rim State Park (UTC 27).

From the intersection of Texas Highway 82 and 87 in southern Port Arthur, take TX 82 east across the dizzyingly high Martin Luther King Jr. bridge, from which you'll have a view of Sabine Lake and its vast bordering marshes (as well as port facilities and petrochemical plants). Where the road loops around and TX 82 turns south toward Louisiana, turn right on T. B. Ellison Parkway.

Continue northeast past the marina, where the road bends right and comes to a T junction. Turn left here and follow the north levee road, which runs for 5 miles to a dead end. You'll have shallow wetlands on your left and the expanse of Sabine Lake on your right. Along the way, on a typical winter day, you may have close views of Common Loon; Pied-billed and Horned grebes; American White and Brown pelicans; Double-crested and Neotropic cormorants; herons and egrets; ducks; shorebirds; gulls; and terns. Though the road is narrow, there are many turnouts (often used by anglers) where you can park and scan the water on both sides of the road. Depending on wind, tide, and luck, birding can be productive or quite slow.

You can also drive the south levee, reached by turning east off T. B. Ellison Parkway 1.2 miles north of its junction with TX 82. This levee road curves around a large impoundment where birds are sheltered from the wind and chop of Sabine Lake. You'll also pass a large area of marsh where bitterns and rails skulk.

If you happen to be on Pleasure Island during spring migration, it's certainly worth taking time to check the live oaks and other trees in some of the recreation areas for songbirds, especially after passage of a weather front with rain and/or north winds.

Pleasure Island
520 Pleasure Pier Boulevard
Port Arthur, TX 77642
(409) 982–4675

Texas Point National Wildlife Refuge and Sabine Woods

On the way to better-known (and, often, more accessible) sites along Texas Highway 87, it can be worthwhile to visit the Texas Point area of Texas Point National Wildlife Refuge. From the town of Sabine Pass, where TX 87 makes a 90-degree turn to the west, drive south 1.4 miles on Texas Highway 3322 (Dowling Road). At the industry-lined strip called South First Avenue, turn right (west) and drive about 1.5 miles to an extensive marsh. Continue along this road as far as you can; it's sometimes flooded and not in good shape, but if it's passable you can often spot waders, waterfowl, and Clapper Rail. At times, migrant songbirds can be seen quite closely in the scrubby salt cedars that line the road.

Return to TX 87 and drive west 2.2 miles to a small parking lot on the south side of the highway. Here Texas Point National Wildlife Refuge (UTC 25; administered by nearby McFaddin NWR) offers a trail leading to another expanse of marsh. You can walk out along a levee if you like (and if the mosquitoes aren't too bad). Again, the shrubs provide a resting place for birds in spring and fall migration. Watch for, and avoid, the mounds of fire ants as you explore.

Continue west along TX 87 about 2 miles. On any day from April to early May, cars from several states will be lined up in the parking lot at Sabine Woods (UTC 26), on the north side of the road. Owned by the Texas Ornithological Society, this relatively small woodland of live oaks and other trees has become a favorite location for birders to search for northbound migrants, and to hope for weather conditions that might create a "fallout" of tired trans-Gulf travelers. (See High Island, UTC 51–55, in the Upper Coast chapter for a discussion of spring migration along the coast.)

Cuckoos, flycatchers, vireos, thrushes, warblers, tanagers, buntings, and orioles can teem in the trees here, or the woods can be fairly quiet when winds and migration patterns conspire against birders. If possible, try to visit Sabine Woods (and other coastal spring migration spots) soon after a storm or passage of a front with northerly winds. Birds may well show up in late morning or afternoon; at times a silent woodland can be transformed into a busy place in a matter of minutes, when northbound birds start dropping from the sky on a schedule that's only theirs.

Paths wind through closed woods and open, shrubby patches. Walk quietly and look and listen, not only for birds but for other birders, who may spot something good in another part of the area. Word gets passed around when an unusual species shows up, and—an advantage of birding in a small, isolated spot like this—such a species often stays long enough that many people can get a look at it. Sharing an observation of, say, a Yellow-bellied Flycatcher or Cape May Warbler is part of the fun of spring birding along the coast.

As is true in similar spots, fall can also be an exciting time to visit Sabine Woods. Birds don't arrive in waves, as they sometimes do in spring, and many are in drabber fall plumage, but they can be present in a similar variety, and the challenge and satisfaction of finding them is just as great.

There are rest rooms at the Texas Point NWR parking lot and at Sabine Woods but no other facilities.

McFaddin/Texas Point National Wildlife Refuges
P.O. Box 609
Sabine Pass, TX 77655
(409) 971–2909
southwest.fws.gov/refuges/texas/mcfad.html

Sabine Woods Sanctuary
www.texasbirds.org/sanctuaries.html

Sea Rim State Park

This gulfside park offers camping, a bathhouse, and 5 miles of beach where kids (and adults) can play and swim. Primitive camping is permitted along 2 miles of the beach, often allowing you to pitch a tent or park an RV in relative solitude, with gulls and terns as your nearest neighbors.

Located on the south side of TX 87, just east of the park headquarters, the three-quarter-mile Gambusia Trail lets birders explore a brackish marsh that's home to a variety of waterbirds. Named for the small mosquito fish that swim beneath your feet, the boardwalk trail loops through thick vegetation and open water where alligators often bask on mudflats. Look carefully along the edge of vegetation for Clapper Rail year-round and Virginia Rail and Sora from fall through spring. Seaside Sparrow is always present, though easier to find when males sing from prominent perches in spring; Nelson's Sharp-tailed Sparrow skulks in the vegetation from fall through spring. You may see both Great-tailed and Boat-tailed grackles here. Nearly any wader found along the coast could appear in the marsh, from the tiny Least Bittern to Great Blue Heron and Great Egret. Few places give such easy access to a marsh, and the Gambusia Trail is worth a walk anytime—though there are days when you wish the mosquito fish had an even bigger appetite for mosquito larvae.

If the beach isn't too crowded with sunbathers and picnickers, spend a little time here checking the shorebirds, gulls, terns, and other waterbirds. Willet, Sanderling, Laughing Gull, and Forster's and Royal terns are always present, along with a constantly changing assortment of other species.

The greater part of Sea Rim's 4,141 acres lies north of TX 87, a tract of marshland where adventurous visitors can rent a canoe and explore along miles of marked trails. Pied-billed Grebe, cormorants, waders, waterfowl, and rails can be seen throughout the year. While this may not be the most productive way to bird on a species-per-hour basis, paddling quietly through the expanse of marsh can be an exciting and rewarding experience. Alligators are common in the marsh, and you might spot a nutria, mink, or muskrat. You can even camp in the marsh on wooden platforms, where you'll hear the croaks, chatterings, and squeals of Pied-billed Grebe, rails, Common Moorhen, and Purple Gallinule throughout the night. The park also offers airboat tours of this area, but these noisy machines tend to frighten away birds before good looks can be obtained.

Whether or not you plan to canoe, in spring and summer visit the park boathouse on the north side of TX 87. Barn and Cliff swallows build their nests under the roof, and in recent years a few Cave Swallows have also nested here.

On the south side of TX 87, west of the main park entrance, a short board-walk loops through a low patch of willows, mulberries, salt cedars, and Chinese tallow trees. In spring and fall this small woodland should be checked for migrant songbirds. It's part of the regular circuit migrant-watchers make on this part of the coast, along with Texas Point National Wildlife Refuge (UTC 25) and Sabine Woods (UTC 26).

Sea Rim State Park
P.O. Box 1066
Sabine Pass, TX 77655
(409) 971–2559
www.tpwd.state.tx.us/park/searim/searim.htm
Admission fee.

The Upper Coast

Port Arthur

GULF OF MEXICO

N

0   Miles   20

73

Winnie

124

High Island

High Island

10

1985

Anahuac NWR

562

562

Rollover Pass

Gilchrist

BOLIVAR PENINSULA

87

GALVESTON BAY

EAST BAY

TRINITY BAY

Smith Point

Abshier Wildlife Management Area

Texas City Dike

Port Bolivar

Bolivar Flats Shorebird Sanctuary

Eastern Galveston Island

Texas City

Galveston

Western Galveston Island

3005

GALVESTON ISLAND

WEST BAY

146

Baytown

La Porte

225

146

Armand Bayou Nature Center

1

45

6

8

610

8

45

610

Houston

8

10

6

6

35

288

36

Angleton

The Upper Coast

Some of the most famous birding destinations in the United States (if not the world) are covered in this chapter—sites that, if they were movies, would have five stars, two thumbs up, and "Don't miss" by their names. Every birder should experience the camaraderie (and, of course, the birds) of a spring day in the little town of High Island. Not far away, Bolivar Flats has gained renown as one of the country's finest sites for waders and shorebirds. Anahuac National Wildlife Refuge ranks among the best birding sites in the national refuge system; it's an especially good car-window birding spot for those with limited mobility.

This section of the Great Texas Coastal Birding Trail makes an excellent destination for a trip that combines birding with other activities, perhaps with a spouse or friend who isn't a dawn-to-dusk birding fanatic. Houston of course has wonderful museums and other cultural attractions, and the island resort of Galveston offers some fascinating and rewarding history alongside its sun-and-sand beach lifestyle.

Late spring through summer isn't the best time to visit this hot and humid part of the world (and the hotels and beaches are full of sunseekers, anyway). But the rest of the year there's always something to see, from fall hawks at Smith Point to wintering waterfowl to the phenomenon of spring migration at coastal woodlots (see the High Island section for a discussion of "fallouts.")

Houston, with its busy international airport, is a favorite entry point for foreign birders coming to the United States to experience our country's best birding. A popular route takes them down the coast to the Rio Grande Valley, then back up through the Texas Hill Country before returning to Houston. (You don't have to be from another country, of course, to make this rewarding loop.)

As you plan your travels in this region, note that Texas Highway 87 is closed from High Island east to near Sea Rim State Park, which translates to a looping route through Winnie as you travel between birding sites on the coast near Galveston and the extreme eastern Gulf Coast south of Port Arthur.

"Candy" Cain Abshier Wildlife Management Area

Look at a map of southeastern Texas and you'll note a triangle of land dividing Trinity Bay on the north from East Galveston Bay on the south. At the tip is the community of Smith Point, site of the most important autumn hawk-watching station on the upper coast.

Migrating raptors, flying generally south and west and reluctant to cross large bodies of water, are naturally funneled by the area's topography to this spot. Each fall, official observers and volunteers gather daily to count passing birds and monitor weather conditions; visitors are welcome to help scan the sky. Conducted by the Gulf Coast Bird Observatory, the Smith Point hawk watch utilizes a 20-foot-high tower overlooking East Galveston Bay and covers the period from mid-August through mid-November.

Of the 50,000 to 100,000 raptors that may pass the site in fall, as many as 80 percent may be Broad-winged Hawk, the small *Buteo* of eastern woodlands. The next-most-common species (though far behind Broad-wings) are Mississippi Kite, Sharp-shinned and Cooper's hawks, and American Kestrel. Observers also regularly see Black and Turkey vultures; Osprey; Northern Harrier; Swallow-tailed Kite; Red-shouldered, Swainson's, and Red-tailed hawks; Crested Caracara; Merlin; and Peregrine Falcon. Peak numbers usually occur in late September.

The hawk-watch site is located within "Candy" Cain Abshier Wildlife Management Area (WMA), which was the first area purchased by Texas Parks and Wildlife with money from its nongame and endangered-species fund. The area's 207 acres encompass coastal prairie and a few small oak mottes (dense, isolated woodlands), where northbound migrant songbirds gather to rest and feed after crossing the Gulf of Mexico. Fall migration can also be a rewarding time to look for flycatchers, vireos, warblers, and other species. Local birders know the WMA as a good place to find wintering Henslow's Sparrow, a species that likes wet grassland.

Texas requires that visitors to its wildlife management areas have either a state hunting license, a Conservation Passport, or a Limited Use Permit. For information, call (800) 792–1112. No permit is required, though, for those simply visiting the hawk-watch site.

Smith Point is easily accessible from Anahuac National Wildlife Refuge (UTC 49), about 20 miles by highway to the east. Don't rush as you drive from one site to another in this part of Texas. So flat is the terrain that when it rains, pastures become marshes, and plowed fields become mudflats. You might spot anything from Roseate Spoonbills to large flocks of shorebirds in the agricultural land along the roads, so take your time and watch carefully.

"Candy" Cain Abshier Wildlife Management Area
10 Parks and Wildlife Drive
Port Arthur, TX 77640
(409) 736–2551

Gulf Coast Bird Observatory
103 West Highway 332
Lake Jackson, TX 77566
(979) 480–0999
www.gcbo.org

Sites UTC 49 & 50

Anahuac National Wildlife Refuge

Anahuac (*ANN-uh-wak*) ranks with the upper coast's mandatory stops almost any time of year. With its East Bay Bayou unit located only about 15 miles from famed High Island (UTC 51–55), it can be part of one of the (potentially) best spring or fall birding days along the entire Texas coast.

Summers are hot, humid, and buggy, but even then visitors can enjoy birds such as Neotropic Cormorant; Least Bittern; Roseate Spoonbill; White and White-faced ibises; Mottled Duck; Clapper and King rails (on the Texas coast these two species can be very difficult to tell apart; don't rely on cheek color); Purple Gallinule; Common Moorhen; Marsh Wren; Painted Bunting; and Seaside Sparrow.

It's fall through spring, though, when Anahuac is most appealing, and birdiest. Wintering geese and ducks abound on refuge fields and ponds, with Greater White-fronted and Snow geese most conspicuous. Look among the Snows for the slightly smaller Ross's Goose, with its rounder head and stubbier bill. More than two dozen species of ducks have been sighted at Anahuac, and most winter days will see a dozen or more types easily found.

At the main refuge entrance (UTC 49) off Texas Highway 1985, a small contact station is often staffed by volunteers who can help first-time visitors. Check the board listing recent sightings and walk through the nearby hummingbird garden before moving on. Like High Island, Anahuac is one of many spots along the coast where you'll often run into a number of other birders. News of good sightings gets passed around, so don't hesitate to stop and chat with other binocular toters or to ask what people crowding around a spotting scope have spotted.

Just to the west, the small patch of trees called "the Willows" is excellent for flycatchers, vireos, warblers, and other songbirds in spring and fall migration. Several miles of good gravel roads run through the refuge, including a one-way route around Shoveler Pond, where you can see waterbirds from egrets to ducks to gallinules. A boardwalk on the west side of the pond provides a good lookout spot.

In spring and fall, all six species of rails found in the United States are present at Anahuac, though they're no less shy here than anywhere else. You'll have to be very lucky to get even a glimpse of a Yellow Rail, and the tiny Black Rail essentially never shows itself in the dense marshes. Other rails sometimes wander out into shallow water or onto mudflats on the edge of marsh vegetation. Early morning and dusk offer the best chances. Check with the refuge about special guided rail walks into the grassland, held in spring; these trips offer the best chance to see rails, including Yellow and, rarely, Black.

If you have time, you'll want to drive all the refuge roads, including the ones that lead south to East Galveston Bay, where you can scan the water for pelicans, waders, gulls, and terns. No matter how intent you are on birds, you're bound to pause several times for looks at alligators, common in the warmer months. In spring, stop often to check rows of roadside trees and shrubs, which may be loaded with migrants. Drier grassland areas can host wintering birds such as Northern Harrier; Short-eared Owl (best seen at dusk); and various sparrows including Le Conte's. The uncommon Sprague's Pipit, something of a Texas winter specialty, has been seen in some refuge short-grass areas.

Walk the levee trail just southeast of the visitor contact station for more chances at shorebirds and other waterbirds. Here, as elsewhere on the refuge, keep an eye out for cottonmouths during warm weather; these poisonous snakes find plenty to eat among the refuge's amphibians and small mammals.

Off TX 1985, about 7 miles east of the main refuge entrance road, you'll reach Anahuac's East Bay Bayou section (UTC 50), known for its migrant shorebirds. Hudsonian Godwit and White-rumped and Baird's sandpipers are just a few of the many plovers and sandpipers that stop to feed in fields managed for their benefit. There's an observation platform here for elevated views of the area, but your car makes a good blind along the roads, as well.

Follow the entrance road south to a parking area and a 1.5-mile trail that runs along East Bay Bayou, where hackberry, persimmon, and other trees create another migrant-songbird spot in spring and to a lesser degree in autumn. Wood Duck and Prothonotary Warbler, both among Texas's most beautiful birds, nest along the bayou, where you may also find Anhinga and both Black-crowned and Yellow-crowned night-herons.

Anahuac National Wildlife Refuge
P.O. Box 278
Anahuac, TX 77514
(409) 267–3337
southwest.fws.gov/refuges/texas/anahuac.html

Sites UTC 52–55

High Island

Like Cape May, New Jersey; Dauphin Island, Alabama; and Patagonia, Arizona; the small town of High Island is a legendary destination for American birders. For decades, spring after spring, people have come here to experience songbird migration. When conditions are favorable, this weeks-long phenomenon can provide as much excitement—and fun—as anything the GTCBT has to offer.

Of the millions of birds that migrate north each spring from Mexico and Central and South America to eastern North America, many island-hop across the Caribbean to Florida, while others follow the Texas coastline. But many fly nonstop across the Gulf of Mexico, a challenging journey for small creatures who burn energy in a hurry. When aided by a south wind, birds may zoom right past the coast and come to rest inland. But when the wind is against them or when storms interfere, they reach the coast tired and hungry, and they stop at the first sight of dry land. When migration and weather coincide, the result can be an event called a "fallout," with birds thronging coastal woodlands, trying to restore their depleted bodies. And there's another factor, too: geography.

Though the Texas coast has a number of important islands, High Island is not one of them. The term *island* has been applied colloquially to several places along the Gulf Coast where huge masses of underground salt have been pushed to the surface by the massive weight of coastal sediments, forming slightly elevated domes in this otherwise flat landscape. The patches of live oaks and other trees at High Island are among the largest in region—and, we humans would assume, among the most prominent and inviting to exhausted birds looking down from the skies.

The Houston Audubon Society owns several tracts of woodland at High Island, including the famed sites called Smith Oaks Bird Sanctuary (UTC 52; 143 acres) and Boy Scout Woods Bird Sanctuary (UTC 55; forty-eight acres). The latter is located on Fifth Street, a few blocks east of Texas Highway 124, and is the best first stop for a birding visit. Volunteers are usually here in spring to answer questions and provide directions to other High Island sites, including Eubanks Woods Bird Sanctuary (UTC 53) and the S.E. Gast Red Bay Sanctuary (UTC 54); rest rooms are available at Boy Scout Woods. Especially on a weekend, there may be dozens of birders looking for cuckoos, flycatchers, vireos, thrushes, warblers, tanagers, and other birds in the trees and shrubs. Some people don't enjoy this much camaraderie while birding, but beginners especially can take advantage of all the eyes and expertise gathered in a relatively small area. Trails meander through the low woodland, some of them boardwalks and others dirt paths.

High Island is a wonderful place for less-mobile birders. At both the Boy Scout Woods and Smith Oaks you'll find bleacher-type seats near watering spots, and it's perfectly possible to sit quietly and watch an ever-changing show of species coming to drink. If you have trouble distinguishing Swainson's and Gray-cheeked thrushes, or Louisiana and Northern waterthrushes, you'll enjoy having others to point out field marks. And it's always fun to share the beauty of even such common species as Scarlet Tanager and Baltimore Oriole.

Smith Oaks borders shallow wetlands where wading birds, including Neotropic Cormorant, Great Egret, and the gorgeous Roseate Spoonbill, nest regularly and can be observed quite closely.

The spectacle of spring migration begins in March and continues through most of May, with the peak usually coming in late April. Different species arrive at different periods, however: Northern Parula and Yellow-throated and Black-and-white warblers are among the earliest migrants, while Olive-sided Flycatcher and Mourning Warbler, for example, arrive weeks later. Every day is different at High Island, and there are no guarantees of a long and varied bird list for your visit. The day after a storm or a front with north winds offers the best chance of a great day.

While spring migration is what made High Island famous, local birders also visit here (and other coastal migrant spots) in September and October to see the same birds heading south to their winter homes. The woods may be nearly devoid of other birders, but not of birds—and the chance of wandering rarities may be even greater in fall.

Houston Audubon Society
440 Wilchester Street
Houston, TX 77079
(713) 932–1639
www.houstonaudubon.org
Donations requested.

Rollover Pass and Bolivar Flats Shorebird Sanctuary

The Bolivar Peninsula is the long finger of land that separates East Galveston Bay from the Gulf of Mexico, with sandy beaches fringing its south side and areas of marsh on the north. It's popular with anglers and the sun-and-fun set, but it also boasts one of Texas's most famous birding locations: Bolivar Flats.

TX 87 runs along the peninsula, the route between High Island (UTC 51–55) and the vacation playground of Galveston Island, which encompasses nearly a dozen sites on the GTCBT. Rollover Pass (UTC 56) is the name given to a spot in the village of Gilchrist, 7 miles southwest of High Island, where a boat channel has been cut through a narrowing of the peninsula. It's worth a quick (or long) stop anytime to check the birds that gather on the mudflats to the north of the "pass" and to scan the Gulf. Pelicans, cormorants, wading birds, shorebirds, gulls, terns, and Black Skimmers may be present in varying numbers, depending on the season, the tide, and your luck the day you visit.

Continue 15 miles toward Galveston. As you approach the town of Port Bolivar (the tip of the peninsula, and the location of the free ferry to Galveston Island), watch for Rettilon Road on the south (opposite Loop 108); it's 3.7 miles from the ferry, for those coming from Galveston. Drive south to the beach and turn right along the sand to a parking area at a barrier to vehicular traffic. This is Bolivar Flats Shorebird Sanctuary (UTC 58), managed by the Houston Audubon Society and a famed location for dozens of species of waterbirds.

The mudflats and marsh of the "flats" formed after the building of the 5-mile-long North Jetty at the entrance to Galveston Bay. The jetty altered the flow of sediment-carrying ocean currents, creating a perfect resting and feeding spot for waterbirds—an inadvertently artificially created habitat that's been growing for the past century. Literally tens of thousands of birds are present here at times. An observation platform allows an overview of the area.

White Pelicans can blanket the shallows from fall through spring, with Brown Pelicans present year-round, though less common. Reddish Egret and Roseate Spoonbill are among the waders regularly seen. Shorebirds gather in flocks comprising thousands of individuals of some species; American Avocets create an especially stunning sight in April, with their rufous heads and necks and black-and-white bodies. More than thirty species of shorebirds have been found here, from Wilson's, Piping, and Snowy plovers to Marbled Godwit to Sanderling to Dunlin. Gulls and terns are always abundant, offering a great chance to practice identification skills on birds of varying ages.

It pays to look up occasionally while you're here. The presence of this many prey species attracts Peregrine Falcons regularly from fall into spring, less often a Merlin. In summer, Magnificent Frigatebirds soar high overhead, and in winter a Northern Gannet may zoom by out to sea.

Seaside Sparrow breeds in the marshy area behind the beach, and Nelson's Sharp-tailed Sparrow winters. At this writing, the Houston Audubon Society is trying to buy more land adjacent to the wetlands to protect the birds that use it for nesting or feeding and to keep development away from the vicinity of the flats. Visitors who enjoy the bird spectacle here should consider a contribution to the society at the address listed.

Plan on a long stay at Bolivar Flats, a spot that appeals on many levels. Casual birders will enjoy the sheer numbers of big, showy birds. Visitors from noncoastal areas will rarely have such an opportunity to study this many shore-birds (a group that presents some identification challenges, e.g., Short-billed and Long-billed dowitchers and the small sandpipers known as "peeps") this closely. Experts can scope the surroundings for rarities such as Masked Booby, Curlew Sandpiper, and Kelp Gull, all seen at Bolivar Flats—though, of course, not to be expected.

Depending on light conditions and the tide level, viewing can actually be better from the North Jetty itself, reached by turning south off TX 87 on Seventeenth Street in Port Bolivar, about a half mile from the ferry. The paved top of the jetty allows walking quite a distance from shore, but use caution as you go.

Houston Audubon Society
440 Wilchester Street
Houston, TX 77079
(713) 932–1639
www.houstonaudubon.org

Historic Galveston

A prosperous port city in the late nineteenth century, Galveston was devastated by a September 1900 hurricane that swamped much of the island on which it sits, killing more than 5,000 people. It was one of the nation's worst-ever natural disasters, and it altered the community's destiny forever. (It also prompted Galveston to build the massive seawall that borders its southern shore.)

The city's past endures in the form of historic districts and wonderful old buildings, well worth exploring in between birding trips or on a rainy day. The downtown area known as the Strand is a National Historic Landmark District, full of nineteenth-century structures, many inventively restored. The street called Strand was known once as "the Wall Street of the Southwest" for its commercial enterprises; it's now lined with restaurants, antiques shops, and art galleries, as is the adjacent Postoffice Street arts and entertainment district. Notable attractions include the splendid Grand 1894 Opera House (409–765–1894); the Texas Seaport Museum and the restored 1877 sailing ship *Elissa* (409–763–1877); "The Great Storm" audiovisual show (409–763–8808), depicting the terrible 1900 hurricane; and the Railroad Museum (409–765–5700), with more than thirty railcars and locomotives.

Three fabulously restored mansions, relics of Galveston's boom days, are known locally as the "Broadway beauties," from their locations on the wide boulevard that runs down the center of the island. All offering tours and well worth visiting, they are the 1886 Bishop's Palace (1402 Broadway; 409–762–2475), the 1859 Ashton Villa (2328 Broadway; 409–762–3933), and the 1895 Moody Mansion (2618 Broadway; 409–762–7668).

Galveston Island Convention and Visitors Bureau
2106 Seawall Boulevard
Galveston, TX 77550
(888) 425–4753
www.galvestoncvb.com

Eastern Galveston Island

The resort city of Galveston, set on the eastern end of a 28-mile-long barrier island, makes a good base for a trip that combines birding with other activities—or for couples in which one partner is less enthusiastic about birding than the other. With its interesting (and tragic) history, museums, restaurants, and beaches, and with accommodations from high-end hotels to bed-and-breakfast inns to inexpensive motels, Galveston has offerings and amenities to please just about everyone. Several excellent birding sites are located on the island itself, and the city is within a relatively short drive of several others.

Summer is not the time to go birding at Galveston. The island is packed with vacationers, and the beaches are crowded with swimmers and sunbathers. And the birds are less interesting, too. But after the summer rush and on through spring, Galveston has much to offer the visiting birder.

Many people making the Texas coastal birding circuit arrive on the island via TX 87 and the free vehicle ferry from Port Bolivar (UTC 58). Laughing Gulls follow the big ferryboats, and pelicans and cormorants perch near the docks at both ends of the short ride. With luck you might spot bottlenose dolphins swimming near the ferry on the way across Galveston Bay.

In spring migration, after your vehicle reaches dry land on the island, drive 0.6 mile on TX 87 (Ferry Road) and turn left on Texas Highway 168 to the Corps Woods at Galveston nature trail (Site UTC 61). This small patch of trees offers a chance—or, if you've just come from High Island (UTC 51–55), another chance—for migrant songbirds, resting here after flying across the Gulf of Mexico. Like other coastal "spring fallout" spots, it can be good for fall migrants, too.

Continue south on TX 87 another 0.7 mile to its intersection with Seawall Boulevard. (If you're arriving in Galveston via I–45 from Houston, simply following I–45 as it becomes Broadway will bring you to Seawall.) As its name implies, this major thoroughfare runs atop a massive seawall built to protect the city after a 1900 hurricane that devastated the island and killed more than 5,000 people in one of the greatest weather-related disasters in American history. Turn left (east) here and drive to the spot where the boulevard ends and you must turn right onto Boddeker Drive. A short distance down this road on your left is the entrance to Big Reef Nature Park (UTC 62), where you can cross over a footbridge to bird a sandy, scrubby area. All along here you'll be seeing pelicans, cormorants, wading birds, shorebirds, gulls, terns, and Black Skimmer.

Following Boddeker Drive will take you to the entrance to a recreation area at East Beach called Appfel Park (UTC 62); there's a charge to enter in the warm months, but in the off season it's free. You're allowed to drive on the expansive beach here, though you should of course be careful to stay on hard-packed sand and watch the tide. Currents and tides are always reshaping this eastern end of Galveston Island, but as you explore you're certain to come across flocks of gulls and terns as well as a variety of shorebirds. It's hardly possible to list all the species that you might find at East Beach, but they range from common birds such as Sanderling and Royal Tern to ultrararities such as Kelp Gull and Elegant Tern. You could see Snowy, Wilson's, Semipalmated, and Piping plovers practically side by side or be able to compare several species of "peep" sandpipers in a single scope view. Brown Pelican, Reddish Egret, Black-necked Stilt, Marbled Godwit, and Caspian and Sandwich terns are just a few of the other birds usually present.

Galveston Island Convention and Visitors Bureau
2106 Seawall Boulevard
Galveston, TX 77550
(888) 425–4753
www.galvestoncvb.com/islandbirding/

Side Trip

Moody Gardens

The three tall glass pyramids of Moody Gardens add an exotic touch to the skyline from many viewpoints around Galveston Island as well as from I–45 as you approach from the north. This expansive complex on Offats Bayou includes a hotel, convention center, giant-screen theater, water park, and many other facilities. Don't dismiss it as just another tourist attraction, though. Two of the pyramids contain well-presented exhibits that visiting birders are almost certain to enjoy.

The ten-story Rainforest Pyramid covers an acre of ground, home to 2,000 species of plants and 175 species of animals from the tropical regions of Asia, Africa, and the Americas. Birds, butterflies, insects, reptiles, and fish live in the trees and pools; just as in the real rain forest, you have to search for many of them, hidden in the foliage or camouflaged in the water. An elevated viewing platform lets you spot species that prefer the canopy level, 50 feet or more above the floor.

Penguins and puffins are among the dwellers in the Aquarium Pyramid, along with thousands of species of fish, mammals, and invertebrates from around the globe. With nearly two million gallons of water in its many tanks, the Moody aquarium is one of the largest, and finest, in the country. Here you can see sharks, seals, eels, colorful fish from tropical seas, and an amazing array of coral and anemones. There's a touch tank with tide-pool species, and there are walkways that let you observe tanks from above, below, and the side. A staff of biologists carries on research on ocean life in cooperation with various universities.

On a rainy day—or even a sunny one—Moody Gardens ranks as a worthwhile stop during your stay on Galveston Island.

Moody Gardens
One Hope Boulevard
Galveston, TX 77554
(800) 582–4673
www.moodygardens.com
Admission fee.

A B&B for Birders

The Mermaid and the Dolphin

Built in 1866 and expanded in 1889 and 1898, this grand Galveston mansion was extensively renovated in the 1990s as a bed-and-breakfast inn. Its eight rooms all have private baths and hot tubs; one suite occupies a separate cottage in the small but lush rear garden.

The owners have contacts with local birders, can direct guests to birding spots on the island, and have a collection of birding and other natural-history books.

The Mermaid and the Dolphin
1103 Thirty-third Street
Galveston, TX 77550
(888) 922–1866
www.mermaidanddolphin.com

Western Galveston Island

Beachfront houses and subdivisions are encroaching into what used to be open space on western Galveston Island, but you'll still find some favorite birding sites here. Among them is a state park with a nice nature trail—a possibly welcome bit of exercise for those who've been standing on a Galveston beach staring at flocks of shorebirds through a spotting scope.

Don't think that you have to arrive at designated sites to begin watching birds. So flat and low-lying are many of the fields on the island that they are essentially part-time wetlands; egrets, ibises, or Roseate Spoonbill might appear anywhere along the roadside. In spring a flock of American Golden-Plovers might be feeding in a closely cropped pasture; in winter, Sandhill Cranes might be resting in the fields. A White-tailed Kite might fly overhead anywhere.

Take Stewart Road west from the city of Galveston. (You can reach it by taking, e.g., Eighty-third Street or Seven Mile Road north from Seawall Boulevard/Texas Highway 3005.) At Eight Mile Road (UTC 66), turn north and drive slowly, checking the wetlands on either side of the road for wading birds. In 1.7 miles turn west on Sportsman Road, again watching for whatever herons, egrets, or ibises might be present. Like the next site, this is a dead-end road.

Back on Stewart Road, continue west 2.7 miles to Settegast Road (UTC 67); turn north, drive 0.4 mile and turn left. The fields here are drier and have short grass that often attracts American Golden-Plover, Long-billed Curlew, and Upland Sandpiper in spring.

The next two Galveston Island sites are primarily good for spring—and to a lesser extent fall—migrant songbirds. Farther west on Stewart Road, watch for Lafitte's Cove subdivision and turn north on Eckert Drive. Drive past the first intersection to a small parking lot on the right, the access to Lafitte's Cove Nature Park (UTC 68). Here, in the middle of an upscale housing complex, a boardwalk winds through a wetland with cattails, willows, Chinese tallow, and oaks. Maintained by a local nature club, it's yet another of the coastal "migrant traps" that can be alive with vireos, warblers, tanagers, and other species, especially the day after a cold front moves through in spring. In 2002 Least Grebe, a species that is expanding its range northward, nested at Lafitte's Cove.

If migrants are good here, you might want to stop at the small woodlot called Lafitte's Grove (UTC 69) on Stewart Road just west of Lafitte's Cove; park in a roadside pullout on the south side.

Stewart Road swings south and meets TX 3005/San Luis Pass Road; turn west and watch for the entrance on the south to Galveston Island State Park

(UTC 70; admission fee). This 2,013-acre park stretches from the Gulf of Mexico across the island to West Galveston Bay. It has suffered some environmental degradation at both ends, though: A 1998 storm destroyed the protective sand dunes along the beach; a restoration project has since partially rebuilt them. Another important project is attempting to restore 1,000 acres of marsh lost to erosion and land subsidence on the north side of the park. Native beds of sea grass are returning here, which is good news for fish and invertebrates as well as birds.

There's usually too much human activity on the state park beach for good birding, though in the off-season a walk might turn up shorebirds, gulls, and terns. Most park birding takes place on the north side of the highway, where the Clapper Rail Trail winds through grassland and marsh, partly on boardwalks elevated above bayous. In spring and fall before beginning the walk, check the oaks near the parking lot for migrant songbirds. White-tailed Kite and Crested Caracara are seen often here; both have nested in the park.

Nesting birds out in the marsh and scrubby grasslands include Pied-billed Grebe; Least Bittern; Mottled Duck; Clapper Rail; Scissor-tailed Flycatcher; Horned Lark; Marsh Wren; Loggerhead Shrike; Common Yellowthroat; Seaside Sparrow; and Eastern Meadowlark. In winter watch for American Bittern; Northern Harrier; Virginia Rail; Sora; Short-eared Owl; Palm Warbler; and various sparrows including Nelson's Sharp-tailed.

Nearly any of the local waders, shorebirds, gulls, and terns might be seen in these bayous or on mudflats. From the observation platform at the end of the trail, scan the bay for loons (winter), grebes, pelicans, cormorants, waders, and waterfowl. Magnificent Frigatebird is sometimes seen in late summer.

Drive west on TX 3005 for 11 miles to reach San Luis Pass (UTC 71), the channel between Galveston Island and Folletts Island, where West Galveston Bay meets the Gulf. Just before the toll bridge over the channel, leave the paved highway and (proceeding carefully) drive toward the pass, paralleling the bridge. There is no real road here, just a maze of informal sandy tracks leading to the water, mostly used by anglers. (At this writing there is some discussion about closing this area to vehicles, although it could still be accessed on foot.) At times thousands of waterbirds—pelicans, waders, ducks, shorebirds, gulls, and terns—can be found in and around this tract of open water, mudflats, and beach, attracted by the same "land's-end" topography as East Beach (UTC 62), 28 miles away. If you choose to explore, be aware that mud and soft sand can bog down your vehicle, and incoming tide can cover what was dry land only minutes earlier. A little caution is all you need, and, depending on conditions, the reward can be one of the birdiest spots on the island.

Galveston Island State Park
14901 FM 3005
Galveston, TX 77554
(409) 737–1222
www.tpwd.state.tx.us/park/galvesto/

FeatherFest

Inaugurated in 2003, Galveston's FeatherFest is set to become an annual April event on this resort island, set at the heart of some of America's best birding locations. The first FeatherFest celebration featured field trips to destinations such as W. G. Jones State Forest (UTC 36), Bolivar Flats Shorebird Sanctuary (UTC 58), High Island (UTC 51–55), and Brazos Bend State Park (UTC 117), as well as island sites such as Big Reef Nature Park (UTC 62). In addition, participants could attend seminars on birding skills and photography workshops or go on bay cruises and kayak trips. Though it's one of Texas's newest nature festivals, considering its wonderful location and the many attractions of Galveston Island, FeatherFest has the potential to become one of its best.

Galveston Island Convention and Visitors Bureau
2106 Seawall Boulevard
Galveston, TX 77550
(888) 425–4753
www.galvestoncvb.com
www.galvestonfeatherfest.com

Texas City Dike

A drive along the Texas City dike is one of the distinctive birding experiences of the Texas coast. Beginners will enjoy the number and proximity of waterbirds, from Brown Pelicans to Willets to loafing gangs of Laughing Gulls and Forster's Terns. Using a vehicle as a blind, photographers can get great close-ups of waders and Black Skimmers. Expert birders brave the chilly winter wind off Galveston Bay to search for unusual loons and gulls.

The dike stretches east from Bay Street at the intersection with Eighth Avenue, on the eastern (bay) edge of Texas City. Called "the world's longest man-made fishing pier," and extending 5 miles from shore out into the bay, the dike at first resembles a small village, with shrimp boats and tumbledown bait shops lining the road. Farther out, anglers cast for saltwater fish while huge seagoing ships pass on the way to and from the port of Houston.

The usual procedure is simply to drive slowly, stopping often to scan the bay and the dike itself for anything unusual among the flocks of waterbirds. On a winter visit, for example, Common Loon; Pied-billed and Eared grebes; American White and Brown pelicans; various herons and egrets; Red-breasted Merganser; Laughing, Ring-billed, and Herring gulls; Caspian, Royal, and Forster's terns; and Black Skimmer will all be common. Depending on the conjunction of tide and wind, rafts of both dabbling and diving ducks might be seen near the dike. Birders are always hoping, of course, for a rarity such as a scoter or Black-legged Kittiwake. Unusual species are seen less often in summer, but typical coastal birds are always present.

Be careful when pulling off the paved road surface; after a rain the roadsides can be muddy, and sand can be soft enough to bog down your vehicle.

The relatively self-contained nature of the dike, as well as the birds' habituation to humans and their vehicles, makes this an excellent place for birders with disabilities to get excellent car-window views.

Texas City Parks and Recreation Department
2010 Fifth Avenue North
Texas City, TX 77590
(409) 643–5990

Space Center Houston

About halfway between Houston and Galveston (and very near Armand Bayou Nature Center, UTC 81), you'll find Space Center Houston, the official visitor center of NASA's Johnson Space Center. As you would expect, high-tech displays abound in this fascinating facility. You can see actual Mercury, Gemini, and Apollo spacecraft, touch a moon rock, experience a space walk in a simulator, and "drive" the lunar rover, among many other activities. The Living in Space gallery demonstrates how astronauts perform routine daily tasks in orbit, and you can "land" the space shuttle in the Feel of Space gallery. Tram tours visit the Johnson Space Center, where (depending on NASA current schedule) you'll learn about astronaut training and activities involving the space shuttle, see the building where spacecraft are assembled, and observe other behind-the-scenes NASA operations.

To visit Space Center Houston from I–45, take exit 25 and drive east about 3 miles on Texas Highway 1. From Armand Bayou, drive west 4 miles on Bay Area Boulevard to Texas Highway 3, drive south 1.2 miles to TX 1, and drive west 1.7 miles.

Space Center Houston
1601 NASA Road 1
Houston, TX 77058
(281) 244–2100
www.spacecenter.org
Admission fee.

Armand Bayou Nature Center

Some of the best birding in the United States lies just a short drive from Houston, the fourth-largest city in the country (after New York, Los Angeles, and Chicago). Of the parks and natural areas within the metropolitan area itself, one of the most noteworthy is this 2,500-acre preserve southeast of the city center. Bordered by NASA's Johnson Space Center, petrochemical plants, and housing subdivisions, this oasis of wetlands, woodland, and grassland serves as an invaluable educational resource for Houstonians as well as a refuge for a variety of wildlife.

From I–45 at Webster take Bay Area Boulevard east 7 miles to the Armand Bayou entrance. At the admissions building you can pick up a map to the 5 miles of nature trails that wind through forest and prairie. Especially in spring migration, don't be in a rush to get to the trails themselves; there can be good birding in the woods and ponds near the nature center's buildings. A boardwalk traverses a swampy area on the way to the education building, a good spot for migrant songbirds and Barred Owl. You could spot a Green Heron or Yellow-crowned Night-Heron in one of the small ponds in the vicinity. Barn Owl has nested in the barn at the historic Martyn Farm, near the education building.

Three nature center trails meander through woodland to approach Armand Bayou, but each differs slightly from the others. The 1.4-mile Martyn Trail passes in part through an area of scrubby thickets; it also offers a viewing blind adjacent to a marshy wetland. The 1.4-mile Karankawa Trail winds under large oaks and into a stand of pines. The boathouse at the end of this trail is a good spot from which to scan the bayou; Wood Duck and Osprey are here year-round, and alligators can be seen in the spring and summer. Look also for various herons and egrets, Black-crowned Night-Heron, and Black-bellied Whistling-Duck. A roost of both Black and Turkey vultures is visible across the bayou.

The 1.2-mile Marsh Trail runs for a distance along Armand Bayou, where shrubs and scrubby trees sometimes allow closer looks at migrant birds than you can get in the taller forest; you'll also have good views over the bayou marsh. This path, which may be partly inaccessible during wet weather, also leaves the woodland, passing alongside its border through the adjoining prairie; the "edge effect" of two contrasting habitats can make this one of the most productive spots in the area.

The 0.7-mile Lady Bird Trail leads out through the prairie to an observation platform. Look for White-tailed Kite, which nests here, and in winter for Northern Harrier cruising low over the prairie grasses. Scissor-tailed Flycatcher, Loggerhead Shrike, and Yellow-breasted Chat all breed. You can walk the mowed firebreaks through the prairie in winter to look for Sedge Wren and sparrows.

The coastal prairie here is a small but important remnant of a habitat that once covered nine million acres of Texas and Louisiana; it's estimated that less than 1 percent of this environment still exists in its natural condition. Bison once roamed this prairie, and the center has a small group of these mammals in a fenced area near Martyn Farm.

Armand Bayou offers a variety of nature programs for adults and children. Early-morning bird walks, night walks, canoe trips, and moonlight cruises on a pontoon barge are just a few of the many activities presented throughout the year.

Armand Bayou Nature Center
8500 Bay Area Boulevard
P.O. Box 58828
Houston, TX 77258
(281) 474–2551
www.abnc.org
Admission fee; closed Mondays.

Side Trip

Houston Museum of Natural Science and Houston Zoo

Located in Hermann Park in downtown Houston (off Fannin Street), the Museum of Natural Science is one of the city's major attractions, with exhibits rewarding for any nature enthusiast. It's easily accessible, just a mile south of U.S. Highway 59—although beware of Houston's notorious rush-hour traffic.

Among the museum's attractions are the Hall of Paleontology, with hundreds of fossils and replica dinosaurs; Farish Hall, devoted to Texas wildlife; Cullen Hall, with the world's finest display-quality collection of gems and minerals; an IMAX theater; Wiess Energy Hall, which uses high-tech displays to survey the oil and gas industry (so important in Houston's history); and the Cockrell Butterfly Center, which houses dozens of species of live butterflies in a three-story glass-walled "rain forest."

Houston Museum of Natural Science
One Hermann Circle Drive
Houston, TX 77030
(713) 639–4629
www.hmns.org
Admission fee.

Hermann Park is also home to the Houston Zoological Gardens, with more than 700 species of animals displayed within its fifty-five-acre grounds. More than 200 birds fly freely in the Tropical Bird House. The zoo is one of the breeding centers for a very special Texas bird, the endangered Attwater's subspecies of the Greater Prairie-Chicken. Your chances of observing this bird in the wild are slim, but you can see it here, where a display explains its lifestyle and the loss of coastal prairie habitat that brought it to the verge of extinction.

Houston Zoological Gardens
1513 North MacGregor
Houston, TX 77030
(713) 533–6500
www.houstonzoo.org
Admission fee.

Prairie to Brazosport

The sites in this chapter may not be as well known outside Texas as some to the east and south on the GTCBT, but they include destinations very popular with local birders. All together, they constitute a region of outstanding diversity, from shore to prairie to lush woodland.

Expanding north and northwest with almost frightening speed, the Houston metropolis threatens to completely engulf the last remnants of adjacent coastal prairie—that is, the part not already destroyed by rice farming. Governmental bodies and an active conservation group are working to protect what's known as the Katy Prairie, buying and restoring grassland and wetlands, home to wading birds, waterfowl, and various songbirds. Like a neck and neck race between suburbs and natural areas, the situation is changing as this book goes to press, with new areas being acquired and access improved to others, while ground is bulldozed for new housing tracts.

You can see natural prairie, too, at Attwater Prairie Chicken National Wildlife Refuge, near Eagle Lake. Though much of its area is off-limits, to protect the critically endangered bird for which it's named, this site is an excellent one for waterbirds, raptors, and grassland species.

Southwest of Houston, Brazos Bend State Park deservedly ranks as one of the jewels of the Texas state park system, a place of wetlands and Spanish moss–draped hardwoods, where Roseate Spoonbills and whistling-ducks perch over lazing alligators. Leading visitors to beautiful but easily overlooked spots like Brazos Bend is reason enough for the GTCBT to exist.

An active volunteer group has helped improve access to two coastal national wildlife refuges, Brazoria and San Bernard, near Lake Jackson, in what's known as the Brazosport area. Both are well worth visiting any time of year. Speaking of diversity: Note that this part of the Texas coast has long ranked among the national leaders in number of species seen on the annual Christmas Bird Count.

Two relatively tiny spots, the community of Quintana and "Magic Ridge" near Indianola, have gained nearly legendary status for their ability to attract rarities. Most of their unusual species are seen by local birders who visit regularly;

Prairie to Brazosport

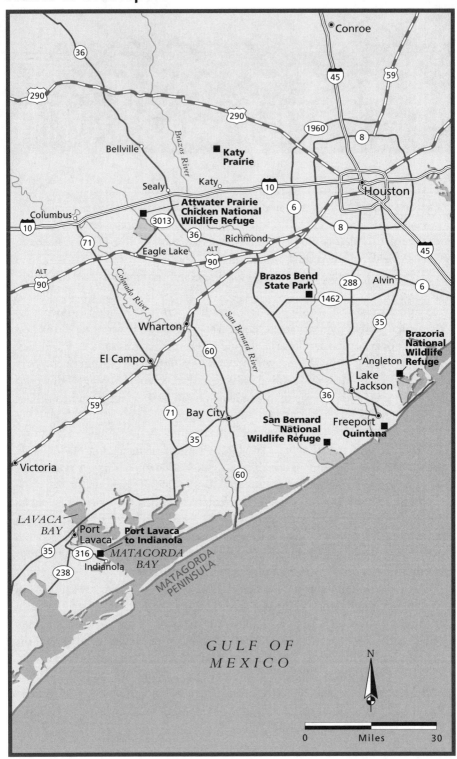

Conroe

36

290

45

59

290

1960

8

Bellville

**Katy
Prairie**

Sealy

Katy

10

Houston

Columbus

**Attwater Prairie
Chicken National
Wildlife Refuge**

3013

6

10

71

36

Richmond

8

ALT
90

Eagle Lake

ALT
90

45

**Brazos Bend
State Park**

288

Alvin

6

Colorado River

1462

35

Wharton

San Bernard River

**Brazoria
National
Wildlife
Refuge**

El Campo

60

Angleton

**Lake
Jackson**

59

71

Bay City

36

35

**San Bernard
National
Wildlife Refuge**

Freeport
Quintana

Victoria

60

*LAVACA
BAY*

Port
Lavaca

**Port Lavaca
to Indianola**

35

316

*MATAGORDA
BAY*

238

Indianola

MATAGORDA
PENINSULA

*GULF OF
MEXICO*

N

0   Miles   30

Brazos River

on any particular day, either place can be devoid of anything special. But uncertainty is part of what makes birding fun. If you want predictability in your hobby, there's always knitting.

Katy Prairie

As the Houston metropolitan area expands, northwestern suburbs swallow up land that once was seasonal wetland and expansive grassland—part of the great coastal tallgrass prairie that stretched from southern Louisiana down through eastern Texas. Less than 1 percent of this environment survives today, making it one of the most endangered habitats encompassed by the GTCBT.

Thanks in large part to farsighted conservationists, representative tracts of prairie have been protected near Houston and continue to harbor wading birds, waterfowl, shorebirds, and other species. The heart of this preservation effort can be found south of U.S. Highway 290, north of Texas Highway 529, and generally west of the road running north and south between the towns of Katy and Hockley. (The road is called in part Katy-Hockley Cutoff Road and in part Katy-Hockley Road.) To visit the Katy Prairie region, drive west from Texas Highway 6 on TX 529 for 8.8 miles to Porter Road and turn north.

NOTE: With a couple of exceptions, this is an area of roadside birding. Much of the land is private, and even the land owned by the Katy Prairie Conservancy conservation group has, at least as of this writing, little public access. Local birders survey it by driving back roads, looking for (often temporary) spots where conditions are right for migrant shorebirds or where a flooded field holds flocks of wintering geese or ducks. A detailed map of the area is a near necessity for extensive exploration. In addition to herons, egrets, geese, and ducks, at various places on the prairie you may see Roseate Spoonbill, Wood Stork, Bald Eagle, White-tailed Hawk, Northern Harrier, Crested Caracara, and Sandhill Crane. When grass conditions are right in spring, you could find migrant American Golden-Plover, Upland and Buff-breasted sandpipers, or Hudsonian Godwit, in addition to more-common shorebirds.

Drive north on Porter Road 1 mile to Longenbaugh Road and turn west. As you approach Katy-Hockley Road in 1 mile, the surrounding flooded fields, called Longenbaugh Waterfowl Pond (UTC 98), may have flocks of wading birds or wintering ducks. This property is scheduled for development, though, so its future as good habitat may be dark.

Turn north on Katy-Hockley Road and drive north 1 mile to Sharp Road. Here, at Paul Rushing Park, Harris County is developing a public nature area with seven lakes, a section of prairie, and handicapped-accessible trails. Incomplete as this book goes to press, this spot will undoubtedly become one of the birding highlights of the Katy Prairie for both wetland and grassland species.

Continue west on Sharp Road (it turns north and then west again) for 3.5 miles to reach an observation platform at the Nelson Farm Preserve (UTC 100), one of the few off-road viewing spots in the Katy Prairie. The adjacent pine woodland is called Barn Owl Woods, and in fact that sometimes elusive species is often found here.

Back at the corner of Sharp and Katy-Hockley Cutoff roads, drive north 1.7 miles on (as it's now called) Katy-Hockley Road and turn right on House and Hahl Road, which zigzags generally north and east about 9 miles to the town of Cypress, on US 290. This road can be good for Bald Eagle, White-tailed Hawk, and Sandhill Crane, among other birds.

Return to Katy-Hockley Road and drive north again. In 1.5 miles you'll cross Cypress Creek, where adjacent wetlands may have wintering waterfowl. Continue north a little more than a mile to Jack Road and turn west. This is an all-around good birding road, although, again, you must bird from the roadside. In 1.8 miles turn north on Warren Ranch Road, where in a mile you'll see the extensive Warren Lake (UTC 99) on the east. Great flocks of wintering waterfowl, migrant shorebirds, and the occasional Bald Eagle can be seen here; in late summer there can be hundreds of herons and egrets. The lake is some distance from the road, though, so a spotting scope is needed for the best viewing. Warren Ranch Road continues north 3.3 miles to Hockley and US 290.

Each year a number of "western" birds are found in the Katy Prairie area, such as Cinnamon Teal; Ferruginous Hawk; Prairie Falcon; Groove-billed Ani; Vermilion and Ash-throated flycatchers; and Harris's Sparrow. Wherever you roam, keep your eyes open for rarities.

Katy Prairie Conservancy
3015 Richmond Avenue, Suite 230
Houston, TX 77098
(713) 523–6135
www.katyprairie.org

Attwater Prairie Chicken National Wildlife Refuge

The bird for which this refuge was named, a subspecies of the Greater Prairie-Chicken found in the upper Midwest, once inhabited a substantial range in the coastal prairie of Texas and Louisiana. Cattle grazing and conversion to cropland destroyed or altered nearly all the native coastal prairie—it's estimated that less than 1 percent remains in a natural state. As the habitat disappeared, so did the prairie-chicken.

A type of grouse, Greater Prairie-Chicken is known for its low, "booming" call notes and, especially, for the male's "dancing" courtship ritual. (Some American Indian dances are believed to have been inspired by the foot-stomping performance of grouse.)

The Attwater's Prairie-Chicken had been extirpated in Louisiana by 1919. By the 1960s, it was in serious decline in Texas, and it was classified as endangered in 1967. Today the only birds known to exist in the wild live in this 10,000-acre refuge and a sanctuary south of Houston. At both locations the populations are maintained only by captive-breeding programs and the release of new, zoo-hatched birds each year. Without such intensive efforts, Attwater's Prairie-Chicken almost certainly would be extinct. Such was the fate of another subspecies, the Heath Hen, which disappeared forever from its range in New England in 1932.

To reach the refuge from I–10 in Sealy, take Texas Highway 36 south about 1 mile, then drive southwest on Texas Highway 3013 10 miles to the entrance road.

Once, it was possible to visit an observation blind here and watch the spring dancing of the prairie-chickens. But several years of bad weather in the 1990s caused the already small population to drop with dismaying speed, and now the refuge tries to protect the birds from all disturbance. The staff can't protect them from all natural enemies, of course; hawks, raccoons, and other predators take many young birds.

Though you're nearly certain not to see an Attwater's Prairie-Chicken at the refuge, its grasslands and wetlands make it a rewarding place to visit. Such specialties as Anhinga; Wood Stork (summer and fall); Fulvous and Black-bellied whistling-ducks; White-tailed Kite; White-tailed Hawk; Crested Caracara; Sandhill Crane (fall through spring); and Painted Bunting (nesting season) are among the highlights. Least Grebe has nested here, and from fall into spring Sprague's Pipit might be found in short-grass areas.

Substantial flocks of geese and ducks winter on the refuge, and with the right combination of water level and season, shorebirds can be abundant on shallow ponds. The 5-mile auto-tour route passes through prairie and along a levee between Teal and Pintail marshes. A good number of birds can be seen from your car, especially from fall through spring. Walking one or both of the refuge's two hiking trails will add to your species list. A winter stroll on the 1.5-mile Pipit Trail might bring a sighting of a Sprague's Pipit or several kinds of grassland sparrows, including Le Conte's; it also passes shallow pothole wetlands. The 2-mile Sycamore Trail winds to the riparian area along the San Bernard River and can be good in spring and fall migration.

To try to re-create natural conditions and restore native prairie species, the refuge burns portions of its acreage each winter, helping kill invasive trees and shrubs. Watch for bison as you drive the tour loop; these impressive mammals have been reintroduced here. Their grazing patterns actually shape grass growth into patterns thought to be beneficial to prairie-chickens.

If you visit on a weekday, stop by the refuge office to talk to the dedicated and knowledgeable staff and to watch a video that explains the sad decline of Attwater's Prairie-Chicken and the efforts being made to bring it back from the edge of extinction.

Attwater Prairie Chicken National Wildlife Refuge
P.O. Box 519
Eagle Lake, TX 77434
(979) 234–3021
southwest.fws.gov/refuges/texas/attwater/index.html

Attwater's Prairie Chicken Festival

Each April the town of Eagle Lake takes special note of its most famous wild neighbor, the critically endangered Attwater's race of the Greater Prairie-Chicken. Cooperating with nearby Attwater Prairie Chicken National Wildlife Refuge (CTC 4), the community sponsors programs about the grouselike bird as well as on other aspects of the Gulf coastal prairie. There are van and walking tours of the refuge, arts and crafts displays, plant walks, and opportunities to meet refuge personnel and other conservationists working to save the Attwater's race of the Greater Prairie-Chicken.

Eagle Lake Chamber of Commerce
408 East Main Street
Eagle Lake, TX 77434
(979) 234–2780
www.visiteaglelake.com

Brazos Bend State Park

One of Texas's most beautiful and rewarding state parks, Brazos Bend is worth a visit anytime—though you might want to avoid summer weekends, when its popularity and proximity to Houston can make for crowds. Covering 4,897 acres, with 3.2 miles of the Brazos River forming part of its boundary, it encompasses 21 miles of hiking trails, seven lakes, a slough, and a good-size creek. Much of its habitat is bottomland forest with live oak, water oak, pecan, and elms; Spanish moss and resurrection fern create a lush, almost tropical atmosphere in the woodlands. Elsewhere the park preserves some remnant tallgrass coastal prairie, dotted with wildflowers from spring through fall.

To reach Brazos Bend from the intersection of Texas Highway 288 and Texas Highway 1462 (20 miles south of Houston), take TX 1462 west about 14 miles to Texas Highway 762, then turn north to the park entrance.

Spring migration can be a great time to visit Brazos Bend, when its forest attracts the usual complement of migrant flycatchers, vireos, thrushes, warblers, orioles, and other songbirds. Its many and varied trails allow easy exploration of different habitats. The Hoots Hollow, Red Buckeye, and Whiteoak trails can all be productive for woodland birds. Among the species nesting in park woods and scrublands are White-tailed and Mississippi kites; Red-shouldered and Red-tailed hawks; Yellow-billed Cuckoo; Barred Owl; Pileated Woodpecker; Acadian, Great Crested, and Scissor-tailed flycatchers; Wood Thrush; Logger-head Shrike; Northern Parula; Prothonotary Warbler; Summer Tanager; and Painted Bunting.

In winter, grasslands such as those around the 0.3-mile Prairie Trail may have Northern Harrier, American Kestrel, Sedge Wren, and half a dozen or more species of sparrows. Crested Caracara is seen fairly often in the park year-round.

For most birders, though, it's the park's wetlands that make Brazos Bend a special destination. With open water, shallow slough, and vegetation-choked marsh, it attracts a wide variety of waders, ducks, and other waterbirds. Take time to walk the 1.2-mile trail around 40 Acre Lake and at least part of the 1.7-mile trail around Elm Lake. A 0.6-mile trail across Pilant Lake connects these two paths, and walking the entire 4-mile circuit will be productive at any season.

Waterbirds breeding at Brazos Bend include Pied-billed Grebe; Anhinga; Least Bittern; Great Blue, Little Blue, Tricolored, and Green herons; Great and Snowy egrets; Black-crowned and Yellow-crowned night-herons; White Ibis; Roseate Spoonbill; Black-bellied Whistling-Duck; Wood Duck; Purple Gallinule; Common Moorhen; and Black-necked Stilt. Many of these are eas-ily seen, swimming in open water or perched conspicuously on lakeside trees. Others, such as Least Bittern and the two night-herons, may require a bit of patient observation to spot. An observation tower at the northeastern corner of 40 Acre Lake lets you scan both it and adjacent Pilant Lake, where many of the aforementioned species breed in mixed heronries.

With winter come species such as American White Pelican, Double-crested Cormorant, American Bittern, more than a dozen kinds of ducks that appear regularly, and an occasional King Rail (here the problem of separating this bird from Clapper Rail, which is found not far away on the coast, is not an issue). Cinnamon Teal is found fairly often, and the rare Masked Duck, a south Texas specialty, has appeared often enough that it's worth keeping in mind. Its cousin Ruddy Duck is fairly common in winter but usually sticks to open water, while Masked prefers to skulk in the vegetation.

Birders with disabilities should note the park's half-mile Creekfield Lake Nature Trail, an interpretive walk that's fully accessible, with a paved path cir-cling a wetland, observation platforms, and benches for rest stops. Park naturalists present a variety of programs throughout the year, including regular bird walks for beginners and advanced birders.

Brazos Bend is known for its alligator population; the big reptiles are usually conspicuous throughout the warmer months. These sluggish-looking creatures can move with surprising speed when provoked, and females can be aggressive in defense of their nests and young. If you see one, keep your distance.

Brazos Bend State Park
21901 FM 762
Needville, TX 77461
(979) 553–5101
www.tpwd.state.tx.us/park/brazos
www.bbspvo.org
Admission fee.

George Observatory

Within Brazos Bend State Park, near the visitor center, you'll find George Observatory, an affiliate of the Houston Museum of Natural Science and one of the region's best and most popular publicly accessible astronomical facilities. A 36-inch telescope is one of three available for public viewing on Saturday nights, weather permitting. Knowledgeable volunteers are present to help beginning stargazers and answer questions. Check the calendar: The Saturday night closest to a new moon, when the sky is darkest, is best for viewing.

George Observatory
One Hermann Circle Drive
Houston, TX 77030
(979) 553–3400
www.hmns.org

Brazoria National Wildlife Refuge

Though this 43,000-acre coastal refuge east of Freeport was established in 1966, only in recent years has it had general public access—thanks in part to the efforts of a local volunteer group, which has funded infrastructure improvements. From Texas Highway 523 about 3 miles north of Oyster Creek, take County Road 227 east 1.7 miles to the refuge sign and gate, then drive 3 miles on a gravel road to the main entrance. (From Texas Highway 35 in Angleton, CR 227 is about 10 miles south via TX 523.) Look for White-tailed Kite, White-tailed Hawk, and Crested Caracara along the way.

At the information pavilion you'll find maps and brochures as well as the trailhead for the Big Slough Trail, a 1-mile nature walk. From a boardwalk across the slough, you may spot Pied-billed Grebe, wading birds, Common Moorhen, Purple Gallinule (spring and summer), and, from fall through spring, various dabbling ducks. The trail continues past the slough, looping through low woods that can be good for migrant songbirds, though the mosquitoes are often so bothersome that you may be discouraged from going far.

A 7-mile auto route runs through grassland and marsh, alongside several ponds. The refuge encompasses a mix of fresh, brackish, and salt wetlands of varying depths, adding to the diversity of birds it attracts. Extensive levees and gates allow refuge personnel to manipulate water levels throughout the year to benefit wildlife. Bitterns, herons, egrets, ibises, and Roseate Spoonbills can be common at times; Wood Storks often appear in late summer, and Sandhill Cranes winter on the refuge. Look for Gull-billed Terns flying over the marshes year-round. Nesting in the cordgrass, bulrushes, cattails, and other wetland vegetation are Clapper Rail (more often heard than seen), Marsh Wren, and Seaside Sparrow; Dickcissels sing their name from atop reeds along the road. While you're looking for these species, in the warm months you're bound to spot alligators, common on the refuge. Keep an eye out for poisonous cottonmouths if you wander away from roads.

From fall into spring, flocks of tens of thousands of geese and ducks rest and feed on Brazoria's marshes and ponds. Greater White-fronted and Snow geese; Green-winged and Blue-winged teal; Northern Pintail; Northern Shoveler; Gadwall; and American Wigeon are among the most common species. Mottled Duck nests here and is present year-round.

A short dead-end road off the main auto-tour loop leads to Rogers Pond, often one of the most productive spots on the refuge for waterbirds. Waders and ducks congregate here seasonally to feed, but local birders know this shallow pond as a great place to see shorebirds in late summer. As the water level declines with summer drought, muddy conditions develop that are perfect for attracting feeding plovers and sandpipers, occasionally in the thousands. This shorebird bonanza may last for only a few weeks in July or August. There's a small observation platform at the edge of the pond, and you can walk along a road bordering the water for a few hundred yards to get a better angle or to put the light at your back.

If you're driving around the refuge auto route in spring, don't forget to check roadside salt cedars and other shrubs for migrant songbirds. Though the available cover is much more limited than at the nature trail, out in the open grassland the wind is often strong enough to keep the mosquitoes at bay.

Brazoria National Wildlife Refuge
1212 North Velasco, Suite 200
Angleton, TX 77515
(979) 849–7771
southwest.fws.gov/refuges/texas/brazoria.html

Sites UTC 121 & 122

Quintana

A tiny woodlot in the beach village of Quintana has developed a large reputation as a place to find rare migrant songbirds in spring and fall and as a rewarding spot to enjoy the usual flycatchers, vireos, and warblers passing through. In addition, a nearby jetty offers a good lookout for seabirds in the Gulf of Mexico.

From TX 36 in Freeport, take Texas Highway 1495 south over the Intracoastal Waterway 1.7 miles to a stop sign at Lamar Street. Turn left (east) and drive 2 miles to the Quintana Neotropical Bird Sanctuary (UTC 121). You can park across the street at the Quintana city hall.

The small patch of Hercules-club, salt cedar, and various shrubs here is known as the best "migrant trap" in the area. Among the rarities that have been found are Mangrove Cuckoo; Western Wood-Pewee; Say's Phoebe; Yellow-green and Black-whiskered vireos; Cape May, Black-throated Blue, Black-throated Gray, Townsend's, and Connecticut warblers; Western Tanager; Pyrrhuloxia; and Cassin's Sparrow. Of course, none of these can be expected on any particular trip, but the sanctuary's position as one of the very few patches of trees in the area makes it a figurative magnet for migrant birds looking for food and shelter. Trails and benches make this an inviting spot to relax and see what drops out of the sky in spring and fall.

Drive east to Fifth Street and turn right (south) to reach Burnet Street and the entrance to Quintana Beach County Park (UTC 122). Cross over the bordering dunes via a boardwalk to reach the beach, where you can look for shorebirds, gulls, and terns. To visit the Quintana jetty, you can walk along the beach or follow Burnet Street east and turn right at Second Street. You can explore out along the 2,000-foot jetty to scan the Gulf of Mexico for loons, Northern Gannet, and scoters, as well as the typical pelicans, ducks, gulls, and terns. Magnificent Frigatebird often soars overhead in late summer. King Eider, Purple Sandpiper, and Lesser Black-backed Gull have been spotted in this area, though, again, all are extremely rare and not to be expected.

There's a fee for access to the county park. An alternative is to leave your car at the sanctuary and walk to the beach via Eighth Street.

Quintana Beach County Park
www.quintana-tx.org/attractions.htm
(979) 233–1461

Migration Celebration

Held in early May in the coastal Brazosport area, south of Houston, this festival features field trips to nearby birding hot spots including Brazoria National Wildlife Refuge (UTC 108), San Bernard NWR (UTC 125), Quintana Neotropical Bird Sanctuary (UTC 121), and Brazos Bend State Park (UTC 117). Trips are also offered to Big Boggy NWR, an area not normally open to the public. Additional activities include children's programs, bird banding, birding seminars, butterfly and dragonfly walks, photography workshops, and varied nature-related exhibits. The festival is coordinated in part by a volunteer group supporting Brazosport's national wildlife refuges.

Southern Brazoria County Visitor and Convention Bureau
159 Brazosport Boulevard
Clute, TX 77531
(800) 938–4853
refugefriends.org

San Bernard National Wildlife Refuge

Grassland, marsh, and woodland combine to offer good year-round birding at this coastal refuge just southwest of Freeport, managed by the same U.S. Fish and Wildlife Service team that oversees Brazoria NWR, a dozen miles northeast. To reach San Bernard, begin at the intersection of TX 36 and Texas Highway 2611 a few miles northwest of Freeport. Drive southwest 4.2 miles on TX 2611 and turn south on Texas Highway 2918. In a bit over a mile, turn west on gravel County Road 306; in less than a mile you'll see the entrance to the refuge headquarters (open weekdays) on the left. The 3-mile Moccasin Pond driving route begins farther west off CR 306.

The 27,414-acre refuge (much of it not accessible to the public) offers several opportunities for exploration. You'll see a lot simply driving the auto-tour route. Waders of more than a dozen species (including Roseate Spoonbill) are always present, and Wood Storks arrive in numbers in summer and early fall. In winter, tens of thousands of Snow Geese make their home here, with lesser numbers of Greater White-fronted, Ross's, and Canada geese. Sandhill Cranes are also common winter visitors.

Nesting Black-bellied and Fulvous whistling-ducks and Wood and Mottled ducks are joined in winter by flocks of ducks of fifteen or more species. Other refuge nesting birds include Least (rare and irregular) and Pied-billed grebes; Neotropic Cormorant; White-tailed Kite; White-tailed Hawk; Crested Caracara; Purple Gallinule; Common Moorhen; Scissor-tailed Flycatcher; Painted Bunting; and Dickcissel. Brown Pelicans and the typical Texas coastal terns breed on wetlands near the Gulf.

You'll see more, of course, by getting out of your car and walking a bit. The Cow Trap Trail follows an old oil well access levee into the marsh, providing a chance to see rails and other wetland species, including the beautiful Least Bittern (spring and summer; uncommon and shy), Marsh Wren, Common Yellowthroat, and Nelson's Sharp-tailed (winter) and Seaside sparrows. Black Rail is said to nest in this marsh; even when present, it's one of the most difficult of all birds to catch a glimpse of, and most birders must be content to hear its *kikee-do* call.

The Bobcat Woods Trail uses a boardwalk to pass through a stand of live oaks, good for songbirds in spring and fall migration as well as for a few nesting species, including Acadian and Great Crested flycatchers, Northern Parula, and Orchard Oriole. The 0.8-mile Scissortail Trail winds through mesquite thickets, where White-eyed Vireo; Loggerhead Shrike; Yellow-breasted Chat; and Indigo and Painted buntings are among the breeders.

In spring and fall and to a lesser extent in winter, shorebirds can be abundant in shallow roadside wetlands. In winter a good variety of sparrows can be found in refuge grasslands.

Except in winter, arrive prepared with plenty of bug juice for the mosquitoes, and keep an eye out for cottonmouths as you walk trails near wetlands.

San Bernard National Wildlife Refuge
Route 1, Box 1335
Brazoria, TX 77422
(979) 964–3639
southwest.fws.gov/refuges/texas/sanbern.html

Port Lavaca to Indianola

Though not so well known as some Texas coastal sites, this area of eastern Calhoun County is a favorite of local birders. Relatively undeveloped (no plastics factories or oil refineries here), it's a place to drive the back roads, looking for whatever shows up, from waders to raptors to migrant songbirds. It also includes a sanctuary called "Magic Ridge" with notable nesting birds, owned by the Texas Ornithological Society.

At the western end of the TX 35 causeway across Lavaca Bay, by the Port Lavaca visitor center, turn south onto Texas Highway 238 and then immediately back east into Lighthouse Beach Park. On your right will be parking for the Formosa Wetlands Walkway (CTC 30), which loops for a half mile through a marshy area on the edge of the bay. Noted as an easy spot to see Clapper Rail (including family groups in breeding season), this small area also has other rails from fall through spring, as well as year-round Seaside Sparrow. On the shoreline and in open water will always be a variety of waterbirds, including American White and Brown pelicans; Double-crested (fall through spring) and Neotropic cormorants; herons and egrets; wintering diving ducks; shorebirds; gulls; and terns. A small covered platform has been constructed here especially for birders.

Continue on TX 238 through the town of Port Lavaca for about 6 miles; take Texas Highway 316 to the southeast. Look for White-tailed Kite, White-tailed Hawk, and Crested Caracara as you drive, and in winter for flocks of

Snow Goose and Sandhill Crane; Wood Stork is regular in later summer in roadside wetlands. In 5.5 miles, turn east on Texas Highway 2760 and drive 1 mile to the community of Magnolia Beach (CTC 31). Follow signs (turning right and left a block) to the beach and North Ocean Drive. Follow this street south 2.7 miles to the town of Indianola and an intersection with TX 316. Along the way Lavaca Bay will be on the east and extensive shallow wetlands and marsh will be on the west. There are many places to park and scan for waterbirds. Be aware that a small number of Glossy Ibis nest with the common White-faced Ibis on a spoil island nearby, so check dark ibises for the former species, here far west of its normal range.

At TX 316 continue south along the beach 0.6 mile to the prominent statue, a monument to the French explorer Sieur de La Salle. Park here to look over Powderhorn Lake (CTC 33), the vegetation-ringed body of water to the west.

Return to the intersection and take TX 316 west, watching in less than 100 yards for Zimmerman Road on the north. Follow it 0.4 miles to the Indianola Old Town Cemetery, a historic site with graves dating from 1851. Park and walk along Zimmerman Road, trying your luck in both directions. The Texas Ornithological Society has purchased 70 acres here as a sanctuary and at this writing is considering acquiring 500 more acres. This area of Tamaulipan scrub vegetation bordered by marsh, called Magic Ridge (CTC 32) by local birders, is known as a nesting site for, among others, Black Rail (in the marshes below the elevated ridge, and of course very difficult to see); Long-billed and Curve-billed thrashers; and Cassin's Sparrow. Other birds nesting in the immediate vicinity include Northern Bobwhite; Gull-billed Tern; Inca Dove; Common Ground-Dove; Greater Roadrunner; Scissor-tailed Flycatcher; Bewick's Wren; Painted Bunting; and Seaside Sparrow. Among the other southwestern-range birds sometimes found in the area (most are rare) are White-tipped Dove; Groove-billed Ani; Ash-throated Flycatcher; Cactus Wren; Pyrrhuloxia; and Olive Sparrow.

In spring and fall the blooming plants on Magic Ridge attract great numbers of migrating Ruby-throated Hummingbirds, and an occasional Buff-bellied shows up as well. The marshes and mudflats on either side of the road can, depending on season and water level, have abundant wading birds and/or shorebirds. Magic Ridge is also a wonderful place to be for the spring songbird migration, when the thick vegetation can shelter flocks of flycatchers, vireos, thrushes, warblers, tanagers, and orioles.

www.texasbirds.org/sanctuaries.html

The Coastal Bend

MATAGORDA BAY

GULF OF MEXICO

ARANSAS BAY

Austwell

Tivoli

Aransas National Wildlife Refuge

Lamar

Fulton

Rockport
Rockport

Aransas Pass Wetlands

Aransas Pass

Port Aransas

Port Aransas

MUSTANG ISLAND

Packery Channel County Park

Padre Island National Seashore

PADRE ISLAND NATIONAL SEASHORE

PADRE ISLAND

LAGUNA MADRE

Goose Island State Park

COPANO BAY

CORPUS CHRISTI BAY

Victoria

Refugio

Aransas River

Hazel Bazemore County Park

Sinton

Corpus Christi
Corpus Christi

Beeville

Mathis

Lake Corpus Christi

Lake Corpus Christi State Park
City of Corpus Christi Wildlife Sanctuary

George West

Robstown

Kingsville

BAFFIN BAY

Drum Point

Kaufer-Hubert Memorial Park

Alice

King Ranch

Riviera

Sarita

Falfurrias

Nueces River

N

Miles

0   30

The Coastal Bend

Several towns along Texas's Coastal Bend take birding very seriously, from a tourism standpoint: Rockport and Port Aransas, for example, have developed local birding sites, promote themselves as birding hot spots, and hold annual bird festivals. Rockport's Hummer/Bird Celebration in September is one of the best-attended such events in the nation. These circumstances quite rightly reflect the richness and popularity of the region as a birding destination.

Thousands of people from Canada and northern states come to southern Texas each fall to escape cold weather, but the most famous "winter Texan" of all is the Whooping Crane, the species that might be considered the star of the central coast. From their summer home in Canada, whoopers return every winter to the area around Aransas National Wildlife Refuge (NWR). Companies in the Rockport area offer special boat tours to see these highly endangered birds—trips that are among the highlights of the GTCBT.

The sites covered in this chapter range from expansive protected areas such as Aransas NWR and Padre Island National Seashore to tiny Blucher Park in downtown Corpus Christi. But this is such a birdy part of the world that opportunities are everywhere. Some highways—for example, Texas Highway 361 from Aransas Pass to Padre Island National Seashore—can be considered one long birding location; waders, shorebirds, gulls, and terns are always present, threatening the concentration of drivers tempted to pull to the side for a Reddish Egret or American Oystercatcher. Texas Highway 285 between Riviera and Falfurrias has long been known as "Hawk Alley," for its White-tailed Kites; Harris's and White-tailed hawks; and Crested Caracaras, but in truth any number of other open-country routes offer similar chances at these and other raptors.

Around Corpus Christi you begin hearing Great Kiskadee shout its name, along with the burry nocturnal notes of the Common Pauraque. Both are signs that you're approaching the semitropical Rio Grande Valley, with its "Mexican" species. But to get there you must cross the brush country of the great Texas cattle ranches—in particular, the mighty King Ranch, bigger than Rhode Island. The birding boom has even affected King Ranch operations: Birding tours are now a regular part of its many enterprises, and in fact it's one of the best spots to see some of the area's specialties, including Ferruginous Pygmy-Owl and Tropical Parula.

Aransas National Wildlife Refuge

For birders not just in the United States but around the world, Aransas has long been synonymous with the Whooping Crane, one of the most famous endangered species on earth. After nesting in northern Canada, the sole traditionally wild flock of these birds flies 2,500 miles south each fall to spend the winter on one small stretch of the central Texas coast—and each winter hundreds of nature lovers (or just curious travelers) take time to see them.

The white, 5-foot-tall whoopers once nested widely in the upper Midwest and Canada; they were rare even in the nineteenth century, though, and were intolerant of human settlement. Their population dropped quickly as agriculture took over the plains, until in 1941 only fifteen birds arrived at their Texas winter home. Aransas National Wildlife Refuge had been established here in 1937, but it wasn't until 1954 that biologists discovered, and protected, their nesting grounds in Canada's Northwest Territories and Alberta.

Extinction seemed inevitable, but the tiny remnant flock slowly increased, their recovery helped by their long life span (about twenty-five years in the wild). In 2002 a flock of 185 Whooping Cranes returned to Aransas and the adjacent coast, representing about sixty-seven mated pairs, plus subadult birds and first-year juveniles.

In the meantime, a second, nonmigratory flock has been established in Florida, and a migratory flock, nesting in Wisconsin and wintering in Florida, is also under development (after a failed experiment to create another migratory flock in the West). There are a number of captive birds at various research facilities.

The cranes spend the winter in family groups at Aransas, mainly on mudflats and in saltwater marshes, where they feed on crabs, clams, and other small animals. Most of the refuge's 70,504 acres is closed to public entry to protect the still critically endangered bird. Though the crane population has been increasing steadily for sixty years, an ill-timed storm or a chemical spill in the Intracoastal Waterway, which passes through the refuge, could undo decades of progress.

With luck, you might spot a Whooping Crane on the refuge, but such sightings are uncommon. The best and easiest way to see the birds is to take one of the commercial boat tours from the towns of Rockport or Fulton, south of the refuge (see subsequent entry). Even without a crane sighting, though, Aransas is still a wonderful place to visit from fall through spring.

Texas Highway 2040 leads south of the small town of Austwell directly to the refuge entrance and the Wildlife Interpretive Center, open daily from 8:30 A.M. to 4:30 P.M. (the refuge itself opens at sunrise). The interpretive center is well worth visiting for maps, advice, and to see mounted specimens of a crane family. Beginners should note that there are many other large white birds found commonly at Aransas, including White Pelican; Great and Snowy egrets; the white form of Reddish Egret; White Ibis; and Snow Goose; don't let your eagerness to see a whooper lead to misidentification.

Just across from the Wildlife Interpretive Center, the short, easy Rail Trail offers a chance to see not only rails in the reeds (though they're always elusive) but also other waterbirds such as Pied-billed Grebe (Least Grebe is found occasionally on the refuge); various bitterns and herons; Purple Gallinule; and Common Moorhen. Watch for alligators in the slough as well.

Aransas's 16-mile auto loop continues south from the interpretive center, soon passing the trailhead for the Heron Flats Trail, at 1.4 miles the longest on the refuge. This walk traverses ridges formed from ancient piles of oyster shells, pushed inland by storms thousands of years ago. It passes through mottes (small woodlands) of coastal live oaks, reaching freshwater marshes and tidal flats where waterbirds and waders are common. Depending on the season, this could be your first encounter with Aransas's infamous mosquitoes, which can be ferocious at times.

Bird Trail 1, as other Aransas woodland sites, is primarily good in spring and fall migration, when the oaks, hackberries, persimmons, mesquites, and other trees can harbor flycatchers, vireos, thrushes, warblers, and other songbirds. Regularly nesting woodland and scrub birds include Inca Dove; Yellow-billed Cuckoo; Ruby-throated and Buff-bellied hummingbirds; Ladder-backed Woodpecker; Scissor-tailed Flycatcher; White-eyed Vireo; Blue Grosbeak; Cassin's Sparrow; Painted Bunting; and Bronzed Cowbird. At Jones Lake, a short walk leads to a marshy wetland offering another chance to see grebes, waders (including Roseate Spoonbill); wintering ducks; and Purple Gallinule.

A 40-foot-tall observation tower, 5 miles from the interpretive center, provides your best chance of seeing Whooping Cranes feeding in the extensive marsh below. The adjacent boardwalk is worth walking, leading through a marsh to the shore of San Antonio Bay, where a number of shorebirds and wetland species are possible. Wood Stork can sometimes be found in late summer or fall. If you have time, 0.9-mile Hog Lake Trail can be one of the best birding walks on the refuge, combining woods, scrub, and wetland for a good variety of species.

The auto route, until now two-way, becomes one-way at the observation tower, looping through scrubby grassland and past small freshwater ponds. This route brings the best chance of seeing raptors including White-tailed Kite; Northern Harrier (fall through spring); White-tailed Hawk (occasional); and Crested Caracara (sometimes found in vulture flocks). Look also for Sandhill Crane (winter); Northern Bobwhite; and Wild Turkey. Pyrrhuloxia is an occasional winter visitor, and a number of sparrow species are found in the grasslands.

White-tailed deer are common on the refuge, and with luck you might spot opossum, armadillo, coyote, raccoon, bobcat, or the small piglike mammal called javelina.

Aransas National Wildlife Refuge
P.O. Box 100
Austwell, TX 77950
(361) 286–3559
southwest.fws.gov/refuges/texas/aransas.html
Admission fee.

Whooping Crane Boat Tours

From late fall to spring, several companies offer boat tours of the area around Aransas National Wildlife Refuge, focusing on showing customers the endangered Whooping Crane. These trips, which leave from docks in Port Aransas, Rockport, and Fulton, are by far the best way to see cranes. While it's possible to see the birds from the observation tower and elsewhere at Aransas, sightings are uncommon; from the boats, they're a near certainty.

The cranes are accustomed to ship traffic on the Intracoastal Waterway and seem unconcerned by the tour boats, which stay far enough away so as to not disturb the family groups usually spotted feeding along the shore. In addition, boat trips are sure to encounter many other species, including loons, grebes, pelicans, cormorants, herons, egrets, ibises, waterfowl, gulls, and terns. Trips last three or four hours and are offered in the morning and occasionally in the afternoon. The larger boats have rest rooms and enclosed viewing areas. Reservations are recommended.

For a list of tour boats, call the Rockport-Fulton Area Chamber of Commerce at (800) 242–0071. Three of the more popular cruises are:

Wharf Cat
(800) 605–5448
www.wharfcat.com

Mustang Nature Tours
(866) 729–2997
www.sandollar-resort.com/mustang

Pisces Charters
(800) 245–9324

Goose Island State Park

Located at the southern end of Lamar Peninsula, 321-acre Goose Island State Park divides St. Charles Bay from Aransas Bay. Just across the former lies the tip of the Blackjack Peninsula, part of Aransas National Wildlife Refuge (though by car the refuge entrance is a half hour from the park).

Very popular with anglers and "winter Texan" campers, Goose Island is most noteworthy to birders as a spring-migration site, where trees and shrubs offer shelter to tired northbound songbirds. Like all such areas, Goose Island's birdiness on a particular day depends on weather (the period right after a frontal passage or rain is best) and luck. Even at the height of migration in April, things can be slow—but it's definitely one of the sites to visit if you're in the Rockport area in spring, because on the right day it can be alive with birds. The park also makes a convenient lookout spot to scan the bays for waterbirds year-round.

From Texas Highway 35 just north of the Copano Bay causeway, take Park Road 13 (Main Street in the community of Lamar) east for 1.4 miles to the park entrance. Beyond the entry station, turn right on Lantana Loop into the campground; stay right until you reach Warbler Way. Turn left (south) and in 50 yards park by the rest rooms. Here the park maintains seed and hummingbird feeders and watering stations, and it can be quite productive to simply sit and wait to see what shows up. Ruby-throated Hummingbird is a common migrant, Buff-bellied is an uncommon visitor, and Rufous and Black-chinned are rare.

Walk back to Lantana Loop, cross it, and you'll reach a trailhead for the Turk's Cap Trail, a 0.6-mile path that passes through a woodland of live oak, colima (prickly ash), yaupon, wax myrtle, and red bay, as well as past some marshy spots and open areas. A great number of birds might be found in migration in these differing habitats. Nesting birds of the park include Pied-billed Grebe (Least is rare); Least Bittern (in marsh vegetation); Black-bellied Whistling-Duck; Inca Dove; Scissor-tailed Flycatcher; Black-crested Titmouse; Bewick's Wren; and Painted Bunting.

Return to the main park road and turn right to the bayfront campgrounds. Shallow marshy areas on the right as you cross the small bridge can be good for waders and shorebirds. Especially at low tide, the shoreline can have a good variety of shorebirds. Turning left where the road divides past the bridge will take you to the park fishing pier, stretching out into St. Charles Bay and offering a good viewpoint for scanning for waterbirds. From it or from the shore, you'll spot a changing array of pelicans, cormorants, waders (including Reddish

Egret and Roseate Spoonbill), gulls, and terns, and in winter loons, grebes, and dabbling and diving ducks.

When you leave the park, turn right on Main Street and drive a few blocks to Beach Road. Turn left and follow it north; you can scan St. Charles Bay from spots along the street. In 1 mile turn left to reach the park's famous "big tree," a live oak estimated to be 1,000 years old, with a limb spread of 90 feet. It's the Texas state champion of its species.

Goose Island State Park
202 South Palmetto Street
Rockport, TX 78382
(361) 729–2858
www.tpwd.state.tx.us/park/goose
Admission fee.

CTC Sites 47, 49–51

Rockport

The small resort town of Rockport has been publicizing itself as a birding destination for quite a while—many years before similar communities began to realize the value of birding tourism. Rockport's Hummer/Bird Celebration (see subsequent entry) is one of the nation's leading nature festivals, and the town publishes its own birding guidebook to local sites, which every visiting birder should buy. (The cost is only $2.00; call 800–826–6441 for information.) The town is a popular base for visitors who've come to the area to see the wintering Whooping Cranes at Aransas National Wildlife Refuge (CTC 37). While none of the sites around Rockport itself is noted for a particular specialty or rarity, the region offers a good selection of typical central-coast birds in accessible locations with many amenities for travelers.

When a new causeway was built over Copano Bay, about 6 miles north of Rockport, the old bridge was left mostly in place and is now known as the Copano Bay State Fishing Pier (CTC 49). Birders can use it to search the bay for wintering loons, grebes, diving ducks, and other waterbirds. The pier can be entered from either end of the new causeway (admission fee). The south segment stretches for more than a mile into the bay; the north segment is shorter.

Driving south on Texas Highway 35, then Business 35, you'll reach the Rockport Demonstration Garden and Wetlands Pond (CTC 50) on the east side of the highway, between Traylor and Colorado Streets (4.7 miles from the causeway). Designed to encourage the cultivation of wildlife-friendly plants, this small area can have lots of hummingbirds (mostly migrant Ruby-throated, with an occasional Buff-bellied, Rufous, or Black-chinned) and butterflies. The short boardwalk into a marsh and the 0.8-mile nature trail can be good for songbirds in spring migration.

While in the downtown area, visit Rockport Beach Park (admission fee), off Business 35 where Loop 70 diverges. This recreation area offers good viewing of Aransas Bay and Little Bay. Part of the park is a bird sanctuary where various waterbirds are always present, including nesting Least Tern and Black Skimmer. Wilson's Plover is sometimes among the shorebirds seen here. The park includes a bird observation platform near nesting areas. Islands in Little Bay host breeding herons, egrets, and terns.

Just south of downtown Rockport, at the corner of First and Church (Loop 70) Streets, you'll find the six-acre Connie Hagar Cottage Sanctuary (CTC 51), named for a legendary Texas birding pioneer. Mrs. Hagar died in 1973 after more than three decades of avid birding and promotion of the Rockport area. The trails through the scrubby vegetation here are a popular stop in spring migration and a good place to meet other birders and exchange information about sightings. The abundant trumpet creeper vine attracts plenty of hummers.

On the east side of TX 35 (not Business 35, also known as 35L) 3.5 miles south of Texas Highway 1069 (1.5 miles north of Texas Highway 188) is a tract of low trees and shrubs called Aransas Woods (CTC 47). Managed by a local nature group, this sanctuary is another of the local spots to check in spring migration, when migrant songbirds can throng the vegetation, especially after the passage of a cold front with rain. Trails (which can be muddy at times) lead from the roadside parking area around a shallow wetland, which adds to the diversity of the site.

If you have time, drive the loop around the west side of Rockport and Fulton composed of TX 1069 and Texas Highway 1781, extending from TX 188 south of Rockport to TX 35 just south of the Copano Bay causeway. This area of pastures, fields, and shallow wetlands is good for wading birds (including Roseate Spoonbill), White-tailed Hawk, and wintering Sandhill Crane. Unfortunately, the speed limit is high and there are not many safe places to pull off the highway. Investigate side roads such as Port Bay Road (off TX 1069, 3.1 miles north of TX 188) and Rattlesnake Point Road (off TX 1781, 2.0 miles north of TX 1069).

Rockport-Fulton Area Chamber of Commerce
404 Broadway
Rockport, TX 78382
(800) 826–6441
www.rockport-fulton.org

Hummer/Bird Celebration

Great swarms of Ruby-throated Hummingbirds travel south along the Texas coast each fall on their way to wintering grounds in Mexico and Central America. Rockport's active birding community entices the birds to pause awhile with dozens of feeders around town as well as plantings of hummer-tempting flowers. On the second weekend after Labor Day, Rockport holds its Hummer/Bird Celebration, now one of the biggest nature festivals in Texas. Hummers (not just Ruby-throated but lesser numbers of Buff-bellied and Rufous) are the focus, though the festival also salutes the town's heritage as a year-round birding destination. There are bus tours to spots with hummer concentrations (which can be truly amazing), birding field trips, boat tours, lectures, workshops, banding demonstrations, and other festivities.

Rockport-Fulton Area Chamber of Commerce
404 Broadway
Rockport, TX 78382
(800) 826–6441
www.rockport-fulton.org

Aransas Pass Wetlands

In connecting the towns of Aransas Pass, on the mainland, and Port Aransas, on Mustang Island, TX 361 traverses a string of natural and artificially created islands on a causeway about 4 miles long. On both sides of the highway are expanses of shoreline crisscrossed by informal roads and tracks, providing access to the water (mostly for anglers).

The beach and nearshore waters along the causeway always host a variety of birds, from the very common—Great and Snowy egrets; Tricolored Heron; Willet; Sanderling; Laughing and Ring-billed (winter) gulls; Caspian, Royal, and Forster's terns—to the somewhat-less-common—Reddish Egret; Snowy, Wilson's (summer), and Piping plovers; American Oystercatcher; Bonaparte's Gull (winter); Sandwich Tern—to a host of other waterbirds, waders, and shorebirds that appear seasonally or reside around the bays.

You can spend quite a while exploring this area at any time of year. Often, using your car as a blind, you can approach flocks of shorebirds, gulls, and terns quite closely. Or you can set up a scope and scan the shore and water, wandering around and from one side of the highway to the other as the spirit (and conjunction of sun and birds) moves you. The unpaved shore can range from hard-packed sand to slippery mudholes, however, so take care where and how you drive.

Be aware that the only crossing from Aransas Pass to Port Aransas is by ferry. Multiple boats shuttle vehicles across the bay on a very short trip, but at certain times (especially in summer) there can be a substantial wait to cross.

Port Aransas

This active resort town sits on the north end of Mustang Island, part of the long line of barrier islands that protect most of the Texas Gulf Coast. In recent years it has begun to promote itself as a birding destination, and the local chamber of commerce is happy to provide information on birding as well as accommodations.

If you arrive by the ferry from Aransas Pass, TX 361 (Cut-off Road) will take you around the west side of downtown. Within a quarter mile of the landing, watch on the west side of the highway for the Paradise Pond sign (just beyond the Paradise Isle motel). During spring or fall migration, stop to walk the very short boardwalk into a two-and-a-half-acre wetland. The willows and Brazilian pepper trees here act as a migrant trap for songbirds, and a Green Heron might be spotted clambering around the low branches. Black-crowned Night-Herons have nested here in the past.

Continue on Cut-off Road 0.3 mile to Ross Avenue, which makes a sharp right turn; it's well marked with a sign to the Port Aransas Birding Center (CTC 57), located a half mile down Ross. Here, adjacent to the city water-treatment plant, you'll find a boardwalk into a substantial cattail marsh, with areas of open water and mudflats. An observation tower provides a longer-range view.

The list of nesting birds you might find here include Least (rare) and Pied-billed grebes; Least Bittern; Black-bellied Whistling-Duck; Mottled Duck; Clapper Rail; Common Moorhen; American Coot; and Black-necked Stilt. Other birds often seen include American White Pelican; Double-crested (winter) and Neotropic cormorants; many waders including Roseate Spoonbill; flocks of wintering dabbling ducks including Cinnamon Teal; Purple Gallinule (migration); and shorebirds. A scope is helpful, but many of the birds are accustomed to watchers and sit or swim unconcernedly near the boardwalk.

Watch the sky for Northern Harrier (winter) and White-tailed Hawk (more common in winter). Swallows can be abundant in migration. Also check the plantings around the parking lot for hummingbirds and butterflies.

Port Aransas County Park, located on the beach at the northeastern corner of Port Aransas, can be entered from Cotter Avenue in the downtown area. You can walk out onto the south Port Aransas Jetty (CTC 58), which extends into the Gulf of Mexico, to look for seabirds. Standing on a jetty with a telescope, scanning the horizon for distant birds, is a somewhat specialized pursuit, but those who take time to do it sometimes spot shearwaters or storm-petrels (rare); Masked Booby (a summer wanderer); Northern Gannet (fairly common in winter); Magnificent Frigatebird (fairly common in late summer, often seen near shore); various diving ducks (winter); or Sooty Tern (rare in summer). The beach at the park is often thronged with flocks of shorebirds, gulls, and terns.

Leaving town to the south on TX 361, watch for an observation platform on the west side of the highway a quarter mile south of Avenue G. Called the Port Aransas Wetland Habitat Park (CTC 59), this viewpoint overlooks a shallow pond with variable water level, which sometimes hosts good numbers of waders, ducks, or shorebirds. Piping Plover is sometimes found here. It takes only a moment to check on the site's condition.

As you drive south from Port Aransas toward Padre Island National Seashore and Corpus Christi, you may pass a number of shallow seasonal wetlands along TX 361. Any or all of these could have flocks of wading birds. The open fields are good places to look for White-tailed Hawk and wintering Sandhill Crane. You'll also pass roads to the east offering access to the beach, where you can scan flocks of shorebirds, gulls, and terns. As always, be careful when driving on the sand.

Port Aransas Chamber of Commerce
421 West Cotter Avenue
Port Aransas, TX 78373
(800) 452–6278
www.portaransas.org

A Celebration of Whooping Cranes and Other Birds

This resort community of Port Aransas, on the northern tip of Mustang Island, celebrates its birder-friendliness with a multi-day festival in mid-February. Boat tours to see endangered Whooping Cranes in and around Aransas National Wildlife Refuge highlight the event, which also includes birding tours by bus, general birding and nature boat tours, lectures, art workshops, and exhibits.

Port Aransas Chamber of Commerce
421 West Cotter Avenue
Port Aransas, TX 78373
(800) 452–6278
www.portaransas.org

Padre Island National Seashore

One of America's great natural areas, Padre Island National Seashore protects 130,454 acres of the longest undeveloped section of barrier island in the world. *Undeveloped* is the key word here: The great majority of the park comprises rarely visited beach, dunes, grassland, and mudflats. Most visitors remain in the area relatively near the visitor center, south of which stretch 60 miles of road-less sand—a ribbon of land with the Gulf of Mexico on the east and Laguna Madre on the west.

(Highly developed South Padre Island, a very different place, should not be confused with this area of North Padre. Birding South Padre is covered under sites LTC 34–38.)

The national seashore is not considered one of the top birding hot spots of the Texas coast. There are no "traps" to concentrate migrant songbirds, and the waterbirds are usually those that can be seen elsewhere. This is certainly not to say, though, that traveling birders should skip it. Birds are here year-round in good numbers and variety (summer is the slowest season and also the most crowded with human visitors), and all the habitats are easily accessible by car. More than 350 species have been seen in the park, which in itself shows the potential of the area. Padre Island is definitely worth exploration, not only for birds but for the pleasures of beachcombing, shell collecting, and simply experiencing one of the most pristine and unpeopled seashores in the country.

As you drive south toward the park boundary and beyond on Park Road 22, proceed slowly and with an eye on the roadside. In winter, Sandhill Cranes congregate in the grassland, and where there are shallow, temporary wetlands, waders and shorebirds may be present. Check telephone poles for hawks, including Harris's and White-tailed. Northern Harriers are common from fall into spring. One of the birding highlights of Padre Island is the autumn passage of Peregrine Falcons; in late September a half dozen of these impressive raptors might be seen in a single day, hunting shorebirds and waterfowl.

Shortly after entering the park you'll note a road to the left to the North Beach area. In summer North Beach is very popular and crowded, although this road does also offer access to the park's 5-mile-long Malaquite Beach, from which vehicles are banned. In the off-season, walking this stretch of shoreline can sometimes be quite a solitary experience, and flocks of shorebirds, gulls, and terns may gather here undisturbed by vehicles.

Not far beyond this side road is the park's Grasslands Nature Trail, on the west side of PR 22. In the warmer months, a common experience here is for hikers to proceed a couple of hundred yards and then retreat to their vehicles because of the vicious mosquitoes. Things are more pleasant in winter, when this three-quarter-mile loop may have a variety of sparrows. Interpretive signs will help you understand the ecology of the barrier island's dune and grassland habitat.

Continuing south, you'll reach the turn to the west to Bird Island Basin on Laguna Madre, the park's most popular birding location. As you drive this side road, watch for wetlands where shorebirds and wading birds congregate. Near the shore are grassy spots where Horned Lark is present year-round; you'll have a chance at wintering Sprague's Pipit (rare) and sparrows. From various access points at Bird Island Basin you can scan the shore, the waters of Laguna Madre, and islands for grebes, pelicans, cormorants, herons, egrets, ibises, Roseate Spoonbill, shorebirds, gulls, terns, and Black Skimmer. Many of these birds nest on islands in Laguna Madre, and with migrants they present a constantly changing array of species throughout the year. In winter, waterfowl can be common just offshore. For all these, a telescope is very helpful.

At the park's Malaquite Beach visitor center you can pick up literature and maps and talk to rangers about nature programs. Here again is access to the 5-mile section of Gulf shore closed to vehicles.

South of the visitor center there are no facilities save for a primitive camp-ground 15 miles south. Vehicles are allowed to drive along the sandy beach beyond the visitor center: The first 5 miles are usually accessible and safe for normal, two-wheel-drive vehicles. Past that point, only four-wheel-drive vehi-cles may proceed. (Speak to a park ranger before driving on the beach under any conditions.) At any time of year the beach will have flocks of shorebirds, gulls, and terns, and by approaching slowly in your car, you can often get quite close. Among the ubiquitous species such as Black-bellied Plover; Willet; Long-billed Curlew; Sanderling; Laughing Gull; and Caspian, Royal, and Forster's terns, you could find dozens of other beach birds, including the trio of small plovers—Snowy, Wilson's, and Piping—often looked for on the Texas coast.

The endangered Kemp's ridley sea turtle nests on Padre Island, thanks to a reintroduction program that brought eggs here from Mexico in the years 1978–1988. In 2002 twenty-three nests were found on the beaches of Padre Island. If you should be lucky enough to spot a sea turtle or signs of a nest, make notes of the exact location and notify a park ranger.

Padre Island National Seashore
P.O. Box 181300
Corpus Christi, TX 78480
(361) 949–8068
www.nps.gov/pais
Admission fee.

Packery Channel County Park

On the north side of PR 22, just east of the JFK Causeway from Corpus Christi's Flour Bluff area to Padre Island, watch for a sign to Packery Channel County Park. It's located right next to a visitor center where you can pick up maps and local tourism information.

The area offers two main birding attractions. First, the small park provides a good lookout point for a stretch of Laguna Madre (the body of water between the mainland and Padre Island) as well as for small islands and mudflats. Pelicans, cormorants, wading birds, shorebirds, gulls, and terns are always present here, and in winter loons, grebes, and waterfowl settle on the bay. A telescope is helpful in scanning the expanse of water.

There are plans to dredge a channel across the barrier island here, creating an opening from Laguna Madre to the Gulf of Mexico, an action that has concerned local conservationists. The channel will increase boat traffic and development and could affect the habitat of shorebirds and waders.

Second, in spring local birders walk among the live oaks and other trees lining the streets of the adjacent community, which serve as another of the many coastal "migrant traps" where northbound songbirds stop to rest and feed. As usual, the period right after the passage of a cold front from the north is best, since the bad weather and unfavorable wind tends to "ground" the birds.

The small oak motte (grove of trees) on the left as you enter the park from PR 22 has been preserved as a bird sanctuary. Turn east on Sand Dollar Drive and left on Maria Isabel to reach a small preserve of the local Audubon Outdoor Club. It features trees and shrubs, a viewing platform, and a constructed pond. Otherwise, you can walk the streets of the community to look for migrants. No matter how rare the bird, though, don't trespass into yards and other private property.

If you visit here during the height of spring migration, you're bound to run into local birders who can provide advice about their favorite locations as well as news of rarities.

Corpus Christi

The largest city, save Houston, on the Texas coast is also the center of one of the birdiest regions in the country. Within an hour of Corpus Christi you'll find Gulf of Mexico bays, beaches, saltwater and freshwater wetlands, woodlands, scrub, and grasslands—and the diverse birds that go with them. The annual Corpus Christi Christmas Bird Count often ranks among the highest in the United States in the number of species seen, in recent years topping 200 on occasion. The city has recently become more involved in promoting nature tourism and offers a birding guide among its other tourist materials.

If you're entering the city from Padre Island, PR 22 leads to the JFK Causeway, crossing Laguna Madre, where you'll find the JFK Causeway Wetlands (CTC 65). The sandy shoreline and mudflats along this road can host many waders and waterbirds, including nesting Wilson's Plover, Least Tern, and Black Skimmer. The highway becomes Texas Highway 358 (South Padre Island Drive) in the peninsular suburb called Flour Bluff. Once you've crossed Oso Bay, take the Ennis Joslin Road exit and drive north. Coming from the west, follow South Padre Island Drive to Ennis Joslin.

About a mile north, on the east side of the road, is Oso Bay Park (CTC 68), which provides access to viewpoints of the body of water for which it's named. If you have plenty of time, stop to check this site. Otherwise, local birders prefer to drive north to the stoplight at Nile Street and visit the Hans and Pat Suter Wildlife Refuge (CTC 69). In this twenty-two-acre park, a boardwalk leads to the shore of Oso Bay, with good viewing of open water, brackish marsh, and mudflats that vary in extent with the tide. Pelicans, cormorants, wading birds, shorebirds, gulls, and terns are always present here, and waterfowl winter on the bay. The small trees can be productive for migrant songbirds in spring. Peregrine Falcons often stop to hunt on migration, and a Crested Caracara may wander in from the nearby golf course from time to time.

Depending on light conditions and where the birds are on the bay, you may want to drive to the campus of Texas A&M University at Corpus Christi, across the water from the Suter refuge. Go north on Ennis Joslin to join Alameda Street and continue to Ocean Drive; turn right to reach the campus. Ask at the entry gate for parking for the university hiking and nature trail (CTC 70). Following the trail leads to viewpoints of the same area seen from the Suter refuge, though you're bound to notice different species with a new angle on the scene.

One of the most famous birding sites in Corpus Christi is Blucher Park (CTC 71) in the downtown area. Visited mostly during spring migration, the small park surrounded by an expanse of urban development attracts cuckoos, flycatchers, vireos, thrushes, warblers, tanagers, orioles, and other birds in numbers disproportionate to its size. To reach it from Texas Highway 544 (which splits into Laredo and Agnes Streets), drive north on Staples Street 1 block (from westbound Laredo) or 2 blocks (from eastbound Agnes) and turn east on Kinney; drive 2 blocks, turn north on North Carrizo, and park along the street.

Trees, shrubs, open areas, and a small creek create microhabitats in Blucher Park; informal trails wind through the area. A local nature club holds guided bird walks on weekends in April at 7:30 A.M. Just across the street is a branch of the Texas state Audubon office, where a bulletin board on the porch reports the latest sightings. (At this writing, plans are in progress to make this office a major regional environmental-education center.)

Northwest of town, Pollywog Pond (CTC 77) is an interesting freshwater wetland that's easily accessible, just a couple of minutes from I–37. To reach it take the Callicoate Road exit (Exit 13A) and drive north 0.2 mile to the intersection at Up River Road. Turn west and drive 0.9 mile to Sharpsburg Road. Look to the northeast for two gates about 100 yards from the road. Drive in and park at either of the gates. The two paths leading into the area, part of the city water-treatment plant, are separated by a creek, but a footbridge joins them a short distance in. There's not just one pond here but several, with open water, dense willows, shrubs, and woodland. Least and Pied-billed grebes; Least Bittern (breeding season); herons and egrets; Black-bellied Whistling-Duck; wintering dabbling ducks; shorebirds; Groove-billed Ani; kingfishers; Great Kiskadee; and Couch's Kingbird (breeding season) are a few of the birds it's possible to see here, and of course the area is excellent during migration.

Corpus Christi Convention and Visitors Bureau
1823 North Chaparral
Corpus Christi, TX 78401
(800) 766–2322
www.corpuschristicvb.com

Texas State Aquarium

Set on Corpus Christi Bay north of the downtown area, the Texas State Aquarium houses 300 species of ocean and freshwater creatures in more than forty habitats, focusing on the life of the Gulf of Mexico. Visitors enter through "waterfalls" (40-foot tunnels that simulate submerging into a watery world) before exploring exhibits ranging from sharks and sea turtles to otters and terns. The aquarium's Islands of Steel tank holds 132,000 gallons of water, depicting the artificial reef of an offshore oil-drilling platform; other displays examine the Gulf's Flower Gardens coral reef, estuaries, and barrier islands, among other environments. Changing daily schedules feature dive shows, feeding times, and a touch tank for hands-on experiences with sharks and rays. Outside, Atlantic bottlenose dolphins swim in Dolphin Bay's 350,000-gallon lagoon.

Texas State Aquarium
2710 North Shoreline Boulevard
Corpus Christi, TX 78402
(361) 881–1200 or (800) 477–GULF
www.texasstateaquarium.org
Admission fee.

George Blucher House

This colorful 1904 Victorian inn sits right across the street from one of Corpus Christi's most productive spring-migration birding sites—named, not coincidentally, Blucher Park (CTC 71). Located downtown a half mile from the Corpus Christi Bay waterfront, the luxurious inn features six elegantly decorated rooms, each named for one of the six children of George Blucher, a member of a prominent early city family. All rooms have private baths, televisions, and telephones. Fresh flowers and elaborate breakfasts are among the amenities. In temperate weather breakfast is sometimes served on the veranda under the oaks, elms, and magnolias that surround the house.

George Blucher House
211 North Carrizo
Corpus Christi, TX 78401
(361) 884–4884 or (866) 884–4884
www.georgeblucherhouse.com

Hazel Bazemore County Park

To reach this small park on the Nueces River, take the Up River Road exit from U.S. Highway 77, a half mile south of I–37. Drive west on Up River Road (which is also Texas Highway 624, though it may not be marked here) for 0.7 mile and turn right at the entrance sign.

The park provides a range of habitat, including fields, marshy ponds, and scrub woodland. There's also a marked nature trail. Regularly sighted species include Neotropic Cormorant; Least Bittern; Black-crowned Night-Heron; Black-bellied Whistling-Duck; Mottled Duck; White-winged and Inca doves; Common Ground-Dove; Groove-billed Ani; Common Pauraque; Buff-bellied Hummingbird; Golden-fronted and Ladder-backed woodpeckers; Great Kiskadee (irregular); Couch's Kingbird; Long-billed and Curve-billed thrashers; Pyrrhuloxia; Painted Bunting; Olive Sparrow (scarce); and Bronzed Cowbird. Southern Texas specialties Green Kingfisher and Green Jay are irregular in their appearances here.

But the park's true attraction—in fact, its national fame—comes from its fall raptor migration. Watchers set up a lookout post on the low bluff overlooking the Nueces and count passing vultures, Osprey, kites, eagles, harriers, hawks, and falcons from mid-August through mid-November. In 1998 nearly a million birds were seen, and in 2002 well over a half-million. The great majority of them (more than 90 percent) are Broad-winged Hawks, the small *Buteo* that nests in woodlands over much of eastern North America.

Also common are Turkey Vulture; Mississippi Kite; Sharp-shinned, Cooper's, and Swainson's hawks; and American Kestrel. Scores of Black Vultures; Osprey; Northern Harriers; Red-shouldered and Red-tailed hawks; and Peregrine Falcons are also counted. In 2002 fifty-seven Swallow-tailed Kites were seen—a record for the site. (The best period for this beautiful raptor is late August.) Many other raptors are uncommon but regular, including White-tailed Kite; White-tailed and Harris's hawks; Merlin; Prairie Falcon; and Crested Caracara. Rarities include Bald and Golden eagles; Ferruginous and Zone-tailed hawks; and Common Black-Hawk.

The peak of Broadwing migration occurs in late September. At this time, more than 100,000 birds have been seen in a single day on many occasions. Needless to say, such a sight ranks among the great birding spectacles in North America.

Visitors are welcome to observe the hawk watch. Upon entering the park, turn left past the office and continue down the hill a short distance to arrive at the observation post.

Hawks also migrate through the area in spring, though not in the concentrated numbers of fall. Sometimes in early April, though, a flock of migrating Broadwings will roost for the night in the woodlands in and around the park, taking off the next morning as the air heats up and slowly circling higher and higher into the sky. Though unpredictable as to occurrence, this gathering is a thrilling sight to see.

The last weekend in September, a festival called Celebration of Flight is held at Bazemore, featuring programs on raptor identification and conservation and demonstrations with live hawks. Local conservation groups set up exhibits, as well, but all activities are subject to a temporary halt if a big flock of hawks comes soaring over.

Hazel Bazemore County Park
P.O. Box 18608
Corpus Christi, TX 78468
(361) 387–4231

City of Corpus Christi Wildlife Sanctuary and Lake Corpus Christi State Park

Diverse habitats make this park and adjacent wildlife area, less than an hour west of Corpus Christi, productive for a wide variety of species: waterbirds on the expansive lake; southwestern birds in the arid brushland; and interesting nesting birds and migrants in the riparian woodland.

From the intersection of Texas Highway 666 and Texas Highway 359 in Mathis, drive south on TX 359 for 4.1 miles and turn west on Park Road 25. Immediately on the left you'll see a small parking lot marked CITY OF CORPUS CHRISTI WILDLIFE SANCTUARY (CTC 79); there's another parking lot a half mile farther down PR 25. From both lots, trails lead into a hackberry-palmetto woodland along the Nueces River.

This pretty area is excellent in migration for all sorts of songbirds. Nesting species include Red-shouldered Hawk; Yellow-billed Cuckoo; Barred Owl; Golden-fronted Woodpecker; Great Kiskadee; White-eyed Vireo; Black-crested Titmouse; Olive Sparrow; and Audubon's Oriole (rare). On the river, look for American White Pelican; Neotropic Cormorant; Anhinga; wintering waterfowl; Osprey in migration; and an occasional Green Kingfisher. Near the dam, which forms Lake Corpus Christi, look for nesting Cliff and Cave swallows.

Depending on your luck, you could spend quite a while in the sanctuary, but eventually you'll want to continue on PR 25 about 1.5 miles to the entrance to Lake Corpus Christi State Park (CTC 80). A bird list is available at the park office (admission fee).

The mesquite trees and other arid scrub vegetation here are home to many species associated with areas to the south and west, making the state park a good place for travelers who aren't heading any farther in those directions. Roads wind around to various camping and recreation sites, and by exploring as many as possible, you could find Harris's Hawk; Crested Caracara; Scaled Quail (rare); White-winged (spring through fall) and Inca doves; Common Ground-Dove; Greater Roadrunner; Groove-billed Ani; Lesser Nighthawk (spring through fall); Common Pauraque; Buff-bellied and Black-chinned (spring through fall) hummingbirds; Ladder-backed Woodpecker; Vermilion (winter), Ash-throated (spring through fall), Brown-crested (spring through fall), and Scissor-tailed flycatchers; Couch's and Western (spring through fall) kingbirds; Green Jay; Verdin; Cactus and Bewick's wrens; Eastern Bluebird; Long-billed and Curve-billed thrashers; Pyrrhuloxia; Painted Bunting (spring through fall); Cassin's and Black-throated sparrows; Bronzed Cowbird; and Lesser Goldfinch.

The park roads provide many viewpoints over Lake Corpus Christi, one of the largest bodies of water in the area (though its extent depends on conditions of rainfall or drought). Look along the shore, in marshy spots, and out across the open water for Least and Pied-billed grebes; pelicans; cormorants; waders; Fulvous and Black-bellied whistling-ducks; and Purple Gallinule. In winter, the lake can host Common Loon, Eared Grebe, and an array of dabbling and diving ducks.

Lake Corpus Christi State Park
Box 1167
Mathis, TX 78368
(361) 547–2635
www.tpwd.state.tx.us/park/lakecorp
Admission fee to state park.

King Ranch

Though the King Ranch is a private, commercial operation, and visits are expensive compared to a state park or wildlife refuge, birders may well want to consider a tour here. Not only will you experience one of the legendary places in the Lone Star State, you'll also have a better-than-average chance of seeing some of the most elusive and sought-after species of the GTCBT.

Founded in 1853, the King Ranch has grown in a century and a half to a truly Texas-size spread: At nearly 1,300 square miles, it's larger than the state of Rhode Island. Cattle are a major business, of course (King Ranch developed the now common Santa Gertrudis breed), but the ranch also raises horses; grows cotton, citrus, and other crops; and sells leather goods and other retail products. The ranch has its own museum at 405 North Sixth Street in the town of (note the name) Kingsville.

Protected from most development for decades, the vast tract of ranch property has been a kind of de facto wildlife refuge. (Hunting is also a King business, but, strictly controlled, it has negligible effect on nongame wildlife.) As a result, several species that are uncommon to rare elsewhere in southern Texas practically thrive on King Ranch holdings. Among them are Ferruginous Pygmy-Owl (the ranch has by far the largest population north of the Mexican border), Northern Beardless-Tyrannulet, Tropical Parula, and Audubon's Oriole.

Ranch naturalists, who are expert birders, offer a variety of tour packages, from half day to full day, on a schedule that varies through the year. In addition, depending on season, the ranch also offers customized tours for small groups, who can spend an entire day focusing on their target species. It's essential to call in advance, and/or check the King Ranch Web site, before a visit to understand the range of options and prices.

A long list of southern Texas specialties and other notable birds are seen seasonally on ranch birding tours, among them Least Grebe; White-tailed Kite; Harris's and White-tailed hawks; Crested Caracara; Wild Turkey; Northern Bobwhite; Sandhill Crane (winter); White-winged (spring through fall) and Inca doves; Common Ground-Dove; Groove-billed Ani; Burrowing Owl; Common Pauraque; Buff-bellied Hummingbird; Golden-fronted and Ladder-backed woodpeckers; Scissor-tailed Flycatcher; Great Kiskadee; Couch's Kingbird; Green Jay; Black-crested Titmouse; Bewick's and Cactus (uncommon) wrens; Long-billed and Curve-billed thrashers; Pyrrhuloxia; Olive and Botteri's sparrows; and Hooded Oriole. Other winter possibilities include Sprague's Pipit, Vermilion Flycatcher, and a variety of sparrows including Spotted Towhee, Lark Bunting, and Clay-colored and Le Conte's.

While birding, you could well also see bobcat, white-tailed deer, and javelina, all of which thrive on the King Ranch. All tours begin at the ranch visitor center, located on Texas Highway 141 west of Kingsville.

King Ranch
P.O. Box 1090
Kingsville, TX 78364
(361) 592–8055
www.king-ranch.com
Fee for tours.

Drum Point and Kaufer-Hubert Memorial Park

These two sites about twenty minutes' drive southeast of Kingsville offer the possibility for large numbers of waders, waterfowl, and shorebirds on Cayo del Grullo, an arm of Baffin Bay, itself a Laguna Madre bay.

To reach Drum Point (CTC 91), begin at the southern intersection of US 77 and Business 77 in Kingsville and drive south on US 77 for 4.2 miles. Turn east on Texas Highway 772 and follow it (through several south and east bends) about 8.8 miles to County Road 2250. Turn east here and drive 2.2 miles to County Road 1132, a somewhat obscure (but paved) road to the north. Follow this road a short distance past an eastward curve to its end at the bayshore. The pavement ends here, but depending on conditions and your vehicle, you may drive north along the shore to Drum Point.

From fall into spring the bay before you may have flocks of pelicans, ducks, gulls, and terns. Southern Laguna Madre is the major wintering location for Redhead, and this species may be present in large numbers along with Lesser Scaup, Bufflehead, Ruddy Duck, and more.

Kaufer-Hubert Memorial Park (CTC 92) is a popular spot with RV campers, anglers, and other recreationists, as well as birders. To reach it from Drum Point, return to CR 2250 and drive east, following the road as it turns south to intersect Texas Highway 628 in less than 2 miles at the community of Loyola Beach. Continue southeast on TX 628 a mile to the bridge over Vattman Creek. Depending on water levels and light conditions, you may want to park here (carefully) to scan the creek and its surrounding mudflats for waders and shorebirds.

Then continue across the bridge to the park entrance on your left. Take the first left turn to a parking area, where a path leads to a birding lookout point. This is a pleasant place to sit and watch the changing array of herons, egrets, ducks, plovers, and sandpipers that frequent the mouth of the creek. On the other side of the parking lot is an observation tower providing a viewpoint of Cayo del Grullo.

Incidentally, *grullo* means "crane" in Spanish. While it's certainly possible to see wintering flocks of Sandhill Cranes in the nearby fields, the early Spanish called many long-legged birds (e.g., Great Blue Heron) "crane."

Kaufer-Hubert Memorial Park
(361) 297–5738 or (361) 595–8591
www.klebergpark.org

The Lower Valley

N

0   20
Miles

GULF OF MEXICO

PADRE ISLAND

LAGUNA MADRE

South Padre Island
South Padre Island

Boca Chica

Port Isabel

Sabal Palm Audubon Center and Sanctuary

100

4

48

Los Fresnos

106

345

77   83

Brownsville

509

Rio Grande

Laguna Atascosa NWR

Hugh Ramsey Nature Park

499

Rio Hondo

Harlingen

83

Arroyo Park
Harlingen Thicket

2

Port Mansfield

186

77

Raymondville

Longoria Unit, Las Palomas WMA

107

281

Estero Llano Grande

Weslaco

88

Frontera Audubon Thicket

Salt Lake Tracts

493

Donna

Alamo

493

907

Valley Nature Center

Edinburg Scenic Wetlands

281

186

Edinburg

336

McAllen

Pharr

281

Hidalgo

115

SANTA ANA NWR

107

83

MEXICO

40

Arroyo Colorado

The Lower Valley

The lower Rio Grande Valley can legitimately call itself the number one birding destination in the United States. Advocates of other areas might dispute the notion, but no one could seriously deny that the Valley has a strong claim to the title. Nearly 500 species (498 at this writing) have been seen in the four counties here: Willacy, Cameron, Hidalgo, and Starr. A number of those birds are found nowhere else in the United States.

Certainly no other region of the country takes birding so seriously as an economic force. From Brownsville to Mission and beyond, cities pitch their promotional efforts to birders (and butterfliers and other nature lovers). They print local birding checklists, maps, and guides, and hold some of the best nature festivals in the country. Even businesspeople with their eyes on the bottom line have begun to realize that nature tourism is a major force in the Valley, and that to keep the tourists coming they must help preserve remaining habitat from the pressures of surging population. With more than a million residents, the lower Valley has for many years been one of the fastest-growing regions in the United States. Thankfully, groups like the Valley Land Fund and the Friends of the Wildlife Corridor are working to protect and restore natural areas here, so that generations to come will have a chance to see Brown Jays and Altamira Orioles, not to mention Blue Metalmarks, Texas indigo snakes, and ocelots.

A major force for conservation is the Lower Rio Grande Valley National Wildlife Refuge, which has as its goal the protection of more than 130,000 acres in Texas's four southernmost counties. The refuge currently has acquired more than 90,000 acres in more than one hundred disjunct tracts from the Gulf of Mexico to Falcon Dam. About 40,000 acres are open to the public; most sites have very limited facilities, trails, and signage. As time passes, though, more tracts will be available to birders, and access and trails will be improved. For information and maps to refuge areas, call (956) 787–3079.

Though the Rio Grande Valley is a relatively small area compared to the entire Texas Gulf Coast, there are so many fine birding sites that this book splits the Valley between two chapters. This chapter covers the lower Valley's eastern section, including such sites as Laguna Atascosa National Wildlife Refuge, Sabal Palm Sanctuary, and the new Edinburg Scenic Wetlands. From Least Grebe to Botteri's Sparrow, the birdlife here is unique in its diversity. Nowhere else in the country can you begin birding in the morning imagining that a Collared Forest-Falcon or a Blue Mockingbird might be waiting down the trail.

Contributing to the exotic feeling created by common residents such as Plain Chachalaca and Green Jay are the flocks of parrots and parakeets that fly around cities such as Brownsville, Weslaco, and McAllen. Their degree of "wildness" is in question, but the Green Parakeets, Red-crowned Parrots, and their relatives are beautiful nonetheless. Roost locations tend to change over time, so your best bet is to check the birding hot line (956–584–2731) and ask local birders.

For notes on developments concerning the new World Birding Center, which will have several sites in the eastern Valley, see the introduction to the next chapter.

Longoria Unit, Las Palomas Wildlife Management Area

Las Palomas Wildlife Management Area (WMA) comprises a series of several state hunting areas scattered through the Rio Grande Valley, primarily set aside for dove hunting (*paloma* is the Spanish word for "dove") but rewarding for nonhunters, too. The Longoria Unit, just minutes from U.S. Highway 77, makes a quick, easy first stop for birders entering the Valley from the north—especially worthwhile for people with limited mobility. From Sebastian (on Business 77, 10 miles north of Harlingen), take Texas Highway 506 west. Where the highway makes a sharp south turn at Texas Highway 2629, continue 1.5 miles on TX 506 and look for a parking area on the east.

A short, paved, wheelchair-accessible trail loops through brushy woodland here—a revegetated area that as recently as 1968 was a cotton field. Longoria stands as an island of restored wildlife habitat, surrounded by agricultural land.

Wildflower plantings attract butterflies, and a couple of water drippers make good spots to sit and wait for birds. Plain Chachalacas are common here, as are typical brushland birds such as White-winged Dove (spring through fall); Golden-fronted Woodpecker; Great Kiskadee; Couch's Kingbird (spring through fall); Green Jay; Verdin; Black-crested Titmouse; Bewick's Wren; Long-billed and Curve-billed thrashers; Pyrrhuloxia; and Olive Sparrow. Hooded Oriole is a possibility.

Dirt roads leading into the areas both east and west of TX 506 offer more opportunity for exploring, but use caution in hunting seasons, when Longoria may be closed to nonhunters. Call the contact number that follows for information about visits here.

To explore the roads and woods at this site, as well as most Texas wildlife management areas, you need some sort of permit: either a hunting license, a Texas Conservation Passport, or a Limited Use Permit. To simply walk the nature trail, however, no permit is required at Longoria.

Longoria Unit, Las Palomas WMA
P.O. Box 3012
Edinburg, TX 78540
(956) 447–2704
Permit required (in part).

The Inn at El Canelo Ranch

Owned by the same family for more than a century and half, this working ranch with Texas longhorns and Charolais cattle has been hosting B&B guests since 1990. While the bird list for the property includes more than 300 species, El Canelo is best known as a nearly certain spot for Ferruginous Pygmy-Owl, a small raptor that's quite scarce in the United States except on private ranches in the southern Texas brush country. Owls often appear right in the yard of the main house, which has five guest bedrooms, all with private baths. Elsewhere on the ranch, roads and trails provide the chance to see typical regional birds such as Harris's and White-tailed hawks; Crested Caracara; White-tipped Dove; Common Pauraque; Buff-bellied Hummingbird; Green Jay; Black-crested Titmouse; Olive Sparrow; and Hooded Oriole. Rates include a gourmet dinner as well as breakfast. El Canelo is located west of US 77 about 10 miles north of Raymondville; contact the inn for directions.

Inn at El Canelo Ranch
P.O. Box 487
Raymondville, TX 78580
(956) 689–5042
www.elcaneloranch.com

Wild in Willacy

Centered in Raymondville, the seat of Willacy County, the Wild in Willacy celebration held each October focuses on all aspects of the region's natural history, from the salt water of Laguna Madre to arid brush country of mesquite and prickly pear. One especially notable feature is a schedule of field trips that allow entry to several private ranches usually not publicly accessible. Boat tours explore the bird-rich destinations of Laguna Madre and Padre Island. Wild in Willacy also encompasses children's activities, butterfly walks, speakers, and other nature-oriented programs and exhibits.

Raymondville Chamber of Commerce
P.O. Box 746
Raymondville, TX 78580
(888) 603–6994
www.wildinwillacy.com

Laguna Atascosa National Wildlife Refuge

Few locations anywhere in the United States offer such excellent wildlife-watching opportunities as does this refuge, in its setting where the thornscrub and grassland of extreme southern Texas meet the shore of Laguna Madre, the shallow body of water separated from the Gulf of Mexico by South Padre Island. Laguna Atascosa's diverse habitats, from open brackish water to seasonal wetlands to prairie to dense woodland, attract a wide array of species; its geographic location means it hosts a mixture of eastern and western types; its coastal setting places the refuge in the path of birds migrating to and from the eastern United States along the Gulf shoreline.

Consider that more than 400 species of birds have been seen at Laguna Atascosa. Many, of course, are rare vagrants; nonetheless, it's obvious that a visit here is a must for anyone exploring the Great Texas Coastal Birding Trail. Note, too, that the refuge's 20 or so miles of roads and good viewpoints make it a fine spot for disabled or less-mobile birders; quite a lot can be seen from vehicle windows.

Reach Laguna Atascosa by driving east from Rio Hondo 14 miles on Texas Highway 106 to a T intersection at Buena Vista Road; turn north into the refuge. The visitor center is well worth a visit, but note that it's closed from June through September and open weekends only in May; the rest of the year it's open every day. (Midsummer is the least productive time to visit the refuge—and it's fiercely hot.)

As fabulous as Laguna Atascosa is for birds, its most famous residents are its cats, especially the beautiful ocelot. Perhaps three dozen of these small, elusive animals live on the refuge, though they're very rarely seen. Jaguarundis—even rarer and more elusive—may also inhabit the refuge, as did *el tigre* itself, the jaguar, decades ago. Exhibits at the visitor center focus on these thrilling mammals, their history, current status, and conservation efforts. You can also pick up maps and bird lists and ask advice of refuge staffers and volunteers.

Two walking paths, the very short Kiskadee and the 1.5-mile Mesquite trails, begin near the visitor center. Some of the refuge's typical birds can be seen here year-round, including Plain Chachalaca; White-tipped Dove; Golden-fronted and Ladder-backed woodpeckers; Great Kiskadee; Green Jay; Black-crested Titmouse; Bewick's Wren; Long-billed Thrasher; and Olive Sparrow. Found in nesting season might be Yellow-billed Cuckoo; Buff-bellied Hummingbird; Brown-crested Flycatcher; Couch's Kingbird; Blue Grosbeak; and Painted Bunting. Northern Beardless-Tyrannulet, Yellow-green Vireo, and Tropical Parula are among the rarities that have been spotted in this area.

Drive west from the visitor center the short distance to Laguna Atascosa (Spanish for "muddy lagoon"), where, depending on season and water level (drought has been a factor lately), you might find American White Pelican; Double-crested and Neotropic cormorants; many species of herons, egrets, and ibises; and varied waterfowl. Wood Storks occasionally show up here in summer. The 1.5-mile Lakeside Trail, which begins at the overlook, passes through drier habitat than the previous trails, offering a chance for Common Ground-Dove; Greater Roadrunner; Verdin; Cactus Wren; and Curve-billed Thrasher.

The centerpiece of a refuge visit is usually the 15-mile Bayside Drive, which makes a large loop through coastal prairie to pass alongside Laguna Madre. Before reaching the one-way section, be sure to stop and walk the 1-mile Paisano Trail, a paved, easy loop that usually produces good birding in dense woodland and grassy openings.

As you (slowly and watchfully) follow the Bayside Drive, look for raptors including Osprey (near water); White-tailed Kite; Northern Harrier (winter); Harris's and White-tailed hawks; and Crested Caracara. Certainly one of the highlights of Laguna Atascosa is its population of Aplomado Falcon, a beautiful bird that was extirpated from the United States decades ago. Thanks to efforts by conservation groups and the U.S. Fish and Wildlife Service, this raptor has been successfully reintroduced into parts of its former range with birds from tropical America and captive-reared individuals. Dozens of pairs of Aplomados now nest in Texas, including several at Laguna Atascosa. Great Horned Owls and raccoons are the major predators on the nests of the falcons, which are often located on artificial structures such as power poles.

Other birds to watch for as you drive through grassland and scrub and past wetlands include Least and Pied-billed grebes; Greater White-fronted and Snow geese (winter); Black-bellied Whistling-Duck; Mottled Duck; Sandhill Crane (winter); White-winged Dove (spring through fall); Groove-billed Ani; Vermilion Flycatcher (winter); Horned Lark; Chihuahuan Raven; Pyrrhuloxia (rare); Botteri's (spring through fall), Cassin's, and Lark sparrows; and Bronzed Cowbird.

Mammals that might appear near the roadside include nine-banded armadillo, black-tailed jackrabbit, collared peccary (javelina), and white-tailed deer. Less commonly seen is bobcat; keep in mind that this small cat is far more likely to show itself than is the ocelot.

Once the drive reaches Laguna Madre, stop often to scan the water for grebes, pelicans, wading birds, waterfowl, and shorebirds. This part of Laguna Madre is known as the winter home for vast numbers of Redhead, though the population of this duck can vary greatly over the season. At times, ducks of a dozen or more species may be present on the bay.

Laguna Atascosa deserves a place among the most valuable and rewarding wildlife destinations in Texas. Plans have been made to expand its 47,000 acres, perhaps by as much as 100,000 acres—a development that would be especially meaningful in a rapidly growing part of the state where suburbia and agriculture destroyed a dismayingly high percentage of natural habitat in the last half of the twentieth century.

Laguna Atascosa
P.O. Box 450
Rio Hondo, TX 78583
(956) 748–3607
southwest.fws.gov/refuges/texas/laguna.html
Admission fee.

The Inn at Chachalaca Bend

Certainly one of the most celebrated nature-oriented lodgings in the Rio Grande Valley, the upscale Inn at Chachalaca Bend offers great birding on its forty-acre surrounding property, which includes a resaca (oxbow lake) viewed from an observation tower. Located just northeast of Los Fresnos via Texas Highway 1847 and Texas Highway 2480 (it's best to call or check the Web site for exact directions), the inn is also less than 15 miles from Laguna Atascosa National Wildlife Refuge (LTC 24), one of the region's top birding destinations. The inn has nine rooms plus a lodge and two casitas (individual cottages), all with private baths and spa tubs.

Trails loop through fourteen acres of natural brushland with Texas ebony and mesquite trees; adjacent grassland features a pond where waders feed. Plain Chachalaca, Ringed Kingfisher, Buff-bellied Hummingbird, Green Jay, and Altamira Oriole are a few of the species seen commonly here.

Inn at Chachalaca Bend
20 Chachalaca Bend Drive
Los Fresnos, TX 78566
(956) 233–1180 or (888) 612–6800
www.chachalaca.com

South Padre Island

South Padre is not to be confused with Padre Island National Seashore (CTC 63), a national park unit of miles of unspoiled beach, located four hours north by road (and not accessible via the island itself). South Padre is lined with hotels, condominiums, and restaurants catering to beach lovers, yet this unlikely setting has something to offer birders, especially in spring migration.

You can start birding as soon as the Texas Highway 100 causeway reaches the island. A paved walkway (LTC 37) curves under the bridge, offering the chance to scan the muddy shore for waders, shorebirds, gulls, and terns. (You will have to park some distance away and walk back to the causeway to access this spot.)

From the intersection of TX 100 and South Padre Island Drive, head north on SPI Drive 4 miles to the island convention center (LTC 35), with its distinctive mural, on the west side of the street. Maps and other tourist information are available here. One of the "gateway" sites of the World Birding Center is planned for this location, which upon completion will provide more birding-specific advice for travelers.

At this writing, the main birding attraction is a 1,500-foot Y-shaped boardwalk that leads across a marshy wetland. All six species of North American rails have been seen here, though you shouldn't expect to see even one on any single visit. All skulk through the thick vegetation, rarely showing themselves. Clapper Rail, common in salt marshes along the Texas coast, is most likely; in migration or winter you could spot (or, more likely, hear) King, Virginia, or Sora. Yellow and Black rails are very rare as well as shy. Other possibilities here are Least Bittern (absent in winter), Marsh Wren, and Common Yellowthroat.

Gulls, terns, and Black Skimmers often congregate on the flats behind the convention center. Plantings around the grounds are attractive to butterflies and Buff-bellied Hummingbirds.

Return to SPI Drive and go 2.8 miles south; turn west on Sheepshead Street 1 block to Laguna Boulevard. A local conservation group, trying to preserve habitat on the island, has acquired land in this residential area, preserving it as the Valley Land Fund Migratory Bird Sanctuary (LTC 36). At this writing, ten lots are being revegetated and are worth checking in spring migration for songbirds, which have few other nearby options for resting and feeding as they travel along the coast.

In spring and especially fall migration, keep an eye out for Peregrine Falcons, which often perch on tall structures such as radio and water towers on South Padre.

Drive south on South Padre Island Drive to TX 100 and continue the short distance south to Isla Blanca County Park (LTC 38; admission fee), which occupies the southern tip of the island. Recreation areas and an RV park take up much of this site, but scrubby patches of trees can host spring migrants. The jetty at the southeastern end of the island offers the chance to scan the Gulf of Mexico for loons, sea ducks, and seabirds such as Masked and Brown boobies (summer), Northern Gannet (winter), and Magnificent Frigatebird (summer and fall).

South Padre Island Convention and Visitors Bureau
600 Padre Boulevard
South Padre Island, TX 78597
(800) 767–2373
www.sopadre.com

A B&B for Birders

Brown Pelican Inn

Beach lovers and those who'd like to enjoy the nightlife and other attractions of South Padre Island, as well as island birding locations, should consider this upscale bed-and-breakfast inn. Set on the Laguna Madre shore of the island 2.6 miles north of the TX 100 causeway, the Brown Pelican Inn is also convenient to sites such as Sabal Palm Audubon Center and Sanctuary (LTC 42) and Boca Chica (LTC 43). The inn's eight rooms, all with private baths, are decorated in American and English antiques. Some have fine views over the bay, especially appealing at sunset. The inn can arrange guided multiday birding tours, visiting sites such as Sabal Palm and Laguna Atascosa National Wildlife Refuge (LTC 24).

Brown Pelican Inn
207 West Aries
P.O. Box 2667
South Padre Island, TX 78597
(956) 761–2722
www.brownpelican.com

Boca Chica

Boca is Spanish for "mouth," as in the mouth of the Rio Grande, which reaches the Gulf of Mexico about 18 miles east of Brownsville. At times, that is, the river actually reaches the Gulf. So depleted is its water by human uses that occasionally the flow simply pools up in the sands of Boca Chica beach.

The drive east along Texas Highway 4 is often a solitary one, through mostly undeveloped grassy flats. It's worth making the trip, in fact, just to see such an unspoiled expanse of the Rio Grande Valley. Some of the land in the area has been acquired by the U.S. Fish and Wildlife Service as one of the many disjunct tracts of the Lower Rio Grande Valley National Wildlife Refuge. You'll begin to see the familiar "flying goose" signs along TX 4 about 4 miles east of the intersection with Texas Highway 511. As time passes, there will be more developments here to make the Boca Chica area more birder-friendly.

Watch as you drive out, passing shallow wetlands and mudflats, for roadside birds such as Reddish Egret; White and White-faced ibises; Roseate Spoonbill; Wood Stork (late summer and fall wanderer from Mexico); Osprey (sometimes present in abundance, perched on telephone poles); White-tailed Kite; Northern Harrier (winter); Harris's and White-tailed (mostly winter) hawks; Crested Caracara; Aplomado (from the population introduced at several southern Texas locations) and Peregrine (fall through spring) falcons; Sandhill Crane (winter); Scissor-tailed Flycatcher (spring through fall); Chihuahuan Raven; and Horned Lark, among many others.

One of the most notable species of the area is Botteri's Sparrow, found in the United States only in small parts of Arizona and extreme southern Texas. To find this somewhat shy and inconspicuous bird, it pays to listen to recordings of its song in advance. Stop often along the grassy areas of TX 4 to listen and look.

The low ridges topped with scrubby trees and agaves are here called lomas, and in spring they can be virtual superhighways for migrating songbirds. To be at Boca Chica when the circumstances of migration and weather create favorable conditions is to experience one of the most exciting birding experiences in Texas. Note that there are inholdings of private property at many places along TX 4, but you can access lomas, beaches, mudflats, and open water by watching for national wildlife refuge signs and walking in along old roads. There may or may not be roadside kiosks with maps and other information posted.

Where the highway reaches the open Gulf of Mexico, you may be able to drive along the beach north or south, depending on your vehicle and the state of the tide and sand. In any event, be careful. The Rio Grande is a couple of miles south of this spot, which is popular with wade-anglers trying to hook red-fish, black drum, or speckled trout. The highly endangered Kemp's Ridley sea turtle nests on the beach in this vicinity.

Regardless of season, the beach always hosts numbers of pelicans, waders, shorebirds, gulls, and terns. Wilson's Plover; American Oystercatcher; Black-necked Stilt; Willet; Gull-billed, Caspian, Royal, Sandwich, Forster's, and Least terns; and Black Skimmer nest in the vicinity. Snowy and Piping plovers are seen irregularly, especially from fall through spring. In winter, especially when there are strong east winds, Northern Gannet might be spotted out to sea. In summer and fall, Magnificent Frigatebird soars over the beach.

Lower Rio Grande Valley National Wildlife Refuge
Route 2, Box 202A
Alamo, TX 78516
(956) 787–3079
southwest.fws.gov/refuges/texas/lrgv.html

Sabal Palm Audubon Center and Sanctuary

Beauty, biological significance, and birds—all combine to make this National Audubon Society preserve on the Rio Grande near Brownsville one of the must-visit destinations in the Valley. At its heart is a thirty-two-acre grove of native sabal palm trees, the most important remnant of an ecosystem that once stretched 80 miles upstream along the Rio Grande. So conspicuous was this tree that early Spanish explorers called the river Rio de las Palmas, or "river of palms." But in the intervening centuries, the species that inspired that name (Texas's only large native palm) has nearly been extirpated north of the Mexi-can border by agricultural and urban development as well as changes in the river's natural flooding cycle.

Palm forest occupies only a small part of the sanctuary's 527 acres, but staff members and volunteers work continually to remove exotic species (the area was once a commercial nursery) and encourage native flora. Present habitats include old fields, native scrub, and regrowing forest as well as the centerpiece, the mature tract of sabal palm and Texas ebony.

The sanctuary is located on Southmost Road (TX 1419), 6 miles east of International Boulevard (TX 4) in Brownsville. At the visitor center you can get advice about trails from the dedicated and helpful staff and learn of recent sightings. Although the visitor center opens at 9:00 A.M., you can walk the trails beginning at 7:00.

Unless there's a special rarity elsewhere, head first for the 0.6-mile Forest Trail, which winds through the main palm-ebony woodland. This path continues to a resaca, or old channel of the Rio Grande (a feature more commonly known as an oxbow lake), where you'll find observation platforms. Connecting paths join the Forest Trail to the 1.1-mile Resaca Loop Trail, which follows the wetland to the north. The resaca, abandoned as the main Rio Grande channel in 1895, varies in water level depending on season and drought conditions. Be sure to walk the Resaca Loop Trail and the connecting Oriole and Vireo Lanes; many of the sanctuary's rare birds have been found in these areas.

Some of the birds you might spot along this or other sanctuary trails are Plain Chachalaca; White-winged (spring through fall), Inca, and White-tipped doves; Common Ground-Dove; Groove-billed Ani; Common Pauraque (rarely seen in daylight); Buff-bellied Hummingbird (check feeders at the visitor center); Golden-fronted and Ladder-backed woodpeckers; Brown-crested Flycatcher (absent in winter); Great Kiskadee; Couch's Kingbird (absent in winter); Green Jay; Black-crested Titmouse; Long-billed Thrasher; Olive Sparrow; and Altamira and Hooded (absent in winter) orioles. At the resaca, watch for Least and Pied-billed grebes; Neotropic Cormorant; Anhinga; a variety of waders and ducks (including Black-bellied Whistling-Duck); Common Moorhen; and Ringed, Belted (winter only), and Green kingfishers. Of course the sanctuary is a wonderful place to be in spring migration, when resident birds are joined by transient flycatchers, vireos, thrushes, warblers, and others.

In recent years, birders have found a tantalizing number of rarities at Sabal Palm, as you would expect in such a fine habitat just across the Rio Grande from Mexico. (In fact, this preserve is the southernmost site of the entire GTCBT.) With luck, you might come across such Valley specialties as Masked Duck, Tropical Kingbird, Yellow-green Vireo, Clay-colored Robin, Tropical Parula, Gray-crowned Yellowthroat, Golden-crowned Warbler, and Blue Bunting. If any of these types have been spotted, rest assured that news will be on the local birding hot line or at the sanctuary office.

On the east side of the visitor center, the 0.4-mile Native Trail connects with the 1.2-mile Via del Rio Trail, both looping to the bank of the Rio Grande. The more open and scrubby habitat here offers a better chance to see raptors as well as Groove-billed Ani, Pyrrhuloxia, and Bronzed Cowbird.

Sabal palm is home to a variety of special plants and animals besides its notable birds. The Texas indigo snake and speckled racer are two unusual snakes known to be here, and the extremely rare and elusive small cat called jaguarundi may occasionally be present. Butterfly watchers know Sabal Palm as one of the Rio Grande Valley's hot spots; there's a large and well-frequented butterfly garden adjacent to the visitor center. Among the unusual plants present are David's milkberry, with small white fruits; brush holly; Barbados cherry; and snake-eyes, with fruits resembling miniature eyes.

Sabal Palm Audubon Center and Sanctuary
P.O. Box 5169
Brownsville, TX 78523
(956) 541–8034
www.audubon.org/local/sanctuary/sabal
Admission fee.

Nature Festival

Brownsville International Birding Festival

The "international" in the name of this Rio Grande Valley festival, held annually in July, derives from the opportunity for participants to cross the border for guided birding trips into northeastern Mexico. Additional highlights are pelagic trips into the Gulf of Mexico to look for wandering seabirds such as shearwaters, storm-petrels, and boobies. Tours of the famed King Ranch (CTC 87) and the beautiful Sabal Palm Audubon Center and Sanctuary (LTC 42) are among the many other field trips. In addition, the festival offers art exhibits, birding seminars, butterfly field trips, and evening lectures.

Brownsville Convention and Visitors Bureau
P.O. Box 4697
Brownsville, TX 78523
(800) 626–2639
www.brownsville.org

Gladys Porter Zoo

Anyone with an interest in natural history (and that surely includes birders) traveling in the Valley should make time to visit the excellent Gladys Porter Zoo in Brownsville. Located at Ringgold and Sixth Streets, 0.3 mile east of Palm Boulevard, its thirty-one acres are home to more than 1,500 animals of 400 species. Main exhibits are arranged in areas representing Tropical America, the Indo-Australian region, Asia, and Africa, which means you'll have close-up looks at birds ranging from flamingos and kookaburras to peacocks and ostriches, as well as spider monkeys, kangaroos, tigers, and giraffes. In addition, there's a herpetarium full of snakes, lizards, and turtles, an aviary where macaws and toucans fly, a bear grotto, and an eagle aerie.

Established with funds from a foundation created by businessman Earl C. Sams of the JCPenney Company, the Gladys Porter Zoo has long been respected for its naturalistic display areas and its research on and breeding of endangered species. It also supports an active educational program for local schoolchildren.

Gladys Porter Zoo
500 Ringgold
Brownsville, TX 78520
(956) 546–2177
www.gpz.org
Admission fee.

Hugh Ramsey Nature Park

Located on Harlingen's busy Loop 499 (Ed Carey Drive), this fifty-acre nature park is a fine resource for local residents and visitors. It's also one of the planned "gateway" sites of the World Birding Center.

To reach it from the intersection of TX 106 and Loop 499, drive south on the latter 0.3 mile and look for the parking lot on the east. From the southern intersection of Loop 499 and U.S. Highway 77/83, drive north on Loop 499 1.9 miles. The park is also only about 2.5 miles south of the Harlingen airport, and so it makes a good spot for new arrivals to stretch their legs—and perhaps see their first Plain Chachalaca or Green Jay.

The local Arroyo Colorado Audubon Society has worked hard to replant the fifty-acre park (once a landfill) with native species such as Texas ebony, huisache (an acacia), retama, honey mesquite, and granjeno (desert hackberry). There's a butterfly garden beside the parking lot, from which interconnecting trails wind through scrubby woodland and open areas. One trail parallels Arroyo Colorado, a good-size creek that flows eastward to empty into Laguna Madre at Laguna Atascosa National Wildlife Refuge (LTC 24). Reeds line the creek in many places, but along the trail, vegetation has been cleared for better viewing. Look here for Black-bellied Whistling-Duck or an occasional Fulvous Whistling-Duck or Ringed or Green kingfishers.

Elsewhere in the park, look for White-tailed Kite; Harris's Hawk; White-winged (summer) and Inca doves; Common Ground-Dove; Brown-crested Flycatcher; Great Kiskadee; Couch's Kingbird; White-eyed Vireo; Verdin; Bewick's Wren; Long-billed and Curve-billed thrashers; Olive Sparrow; and Bronzed Cowbird.

In the future, Ramsey Park may be connected via a hike-bike trail along Arroyo Colorado with Arroyo Park and the Harlingen Thicket (LTC 27–28), about 1.5 miles southwest.

Harlingen Area Chamber of Commerce
311 East Tyler
Harlingen, TX 78550
(956) 423–5440
www.harlingen.com

Arroyo Colorado Audubon Society
www.kiskadee.org

Arroyo Park and Harlingen Thicket

These two sites flank Arroyo Colorado, the waterway that bisects southern Harlingen. The park, a popular recreation area, is for birders mostly the access point for Harlingen Thicket and a hike-bike trail that runs alongside Arroyo Colorado. The thicket, an area of scrubby woodland, is good for the same birds found at Hugh Ramsey Nature Park (LTC 26) farther downstream. To reach Arroyo Park (LTC 27), drive north on Loop 499 (Ed Carey Drive) from US 77/83 for 0.5 mile to Hale Street. Turn west and drive 0.5 mile to Hampshire Street; jog right and the parking lot will be on the left. (Hale Street is about 1.5 miles south of Hugh Ramsey Nature Park.)

A paved path leads to an overlook at Arroyo Colorado and to the city hike-bike trail paralleling the creek. Below, a footbridge allows crossing to Harlingen Thicket (LTC 28), forty acres of natural scrub with many typical Rio Grande Valley birds. The thicket is also an excellent spot to check during spring migration, when it offers refuge for northbound songbirds, including flycatchers, vireos, thrushes, and warblers.

A stroll along the hiking path might turn up a Ringed Kingfisher or the small Green Kingfisher, the latter usually spotted perched low near the water or as a quick flash of green as it flits by. Belted Kingfisher also may be seen in winter.

Couch's Kingbird is a common species throughout the Rio Grande Valley, but the look-alike Tropical Kingbird is seen with increasing frequency—or, rather, *heard* frequently, since voice is by far the most reliable way to tell these species apart. Couch's gives a raspy *breeer* call, while the Tropical's voice is a quick *pip-pip-pip-pip-pip*.

One reliable spot to find Tropical Kingbird in recent years has been the Rancho Viejo development, just off US 77/83 about 12 miles southeast of Harlingen. (Look for the giant "golf ball" water tank.) Tropicals nest around the golf course. The species is expanding its range, though, so listen for them wherever you go in the lower Valley.

Harlingen Area Chamber of Commerce
311 East Tyler
Harlingen, TX 78550
(956) 423–5440
www.harlingen.com

Arroyo Colorado Audubon Society
www.kiskadee.org

Rio Grande Valley Birding Festival

With a name like that, it has to be good—and it is. One of the top birding events in the country, this popular Harlingen festival brings in nationally known speakers and offers field trips to the Valley's best birding spots, including Rio Grande boat trips. Experts present programs on identification and varied aspects of ornithology, and there's a Birder's Bazaar of optics and other birding products. This four-day festival in early November is a great way to get acquainted with the birds of one of the county's most famous destinations.

> Rio Grande Valley Birding Festival
> P.O. Box 3162
> Harlingen, TX 78551
> (800) 531–7346
> www.rgvbirdfest.com

Vieh's Bed and Breakfast

Quite a few south Texas specialty birds can be found on the fifteen-acre grounds of this family home about 6 miles south of Harlingen. To reach it, take Texas Highway 509 south from US 77 for 5.5 miles and turn west on Texas Highway 675; look for the entrance on the north side of the highway. Vieh's has four bedrooms, two with private baths, and a separate cottage. Two butterfly gardens have been planted on the grounds, where about 150 species of birds have been sighted. Among the regulars are White-tipped Dove, Barn Owl (nests nearby), Buff-bellied Hummingbird, Great Kiskadee, Green Jay, and Hooded and Altamira orioles.

It's a short walk to the ten-acre pond behind the house, where Black-bellied Whistling-Ducks nest and various herons and egrets and Ringed and Green kingfishers are often seen. Shorebirds pause here in migration, and even Wood Stork and Roseate Spoonbill have been spotted.

> Vieh's Bed and Breakfast
> 18413 Landrum Park Road (TX 675)
> San Benito, TX 78586
> (956) 425–4651
> www.vieh.com

Estero Llano Grande

This site south of Weslaco, one of the "resource" sites of the World Birding Center, is just beginning to be developed at this writing. It's included in this guide because of its excellent potential. To reach it, take the Texas Highway 1015 exit from U.S. Highway 83 (between Weslaco and Mercedes) and drive south about 2.8 miles. The combination state park and birding site will be on the east side of TX 1015. It's located only minutes from both the Valley Nature Center (LTC 57) and the Frontera Audubon Thicket (LTC 58).

Birders will have access here to Estero Llano Grande, a shallow stream that's part of the drainage system connecting to Arroyo Colorado and to newly constructed wetlands. It's also planned that adjacent woodland will be part of the site, adding to the birding diversity.

In the past, the estero has been a good spot for varied waterbirds, including American White Pelican; Neotropic Cormorant; most of the local herons and egrets; occasional Roseate Spoonbill; Fulvous Whistling-Duck and many other duck species; and migrant and wintering shorebirds. With additional wetlands being managed for birding, the possibilities can only improve.

The site's woodland, surrounded as it is by agricultural tracts, is bound to be highly attractive to migrants, as well as home to typical Valley birds from Plain Chachalaca to Couch's Kingbird to Green Jay.

While it's impossible to predict exactly the birding opportunities here, if planned developments occur, Estero Llano Grande is likely to be one of the must-visit sites of the Valley.

(956) 584–9156
www.worldbirdingcenter.org

Frontera Audubon Thicket

Operated by the local Audubon Society, this "thicket" just south of downtown Weslaco is yet another of the many patches of woods in the Rio Grande Valley that local birders and visitors frequent for resident and migrant species—and in hopes of rarities. The Weslaco thicket commanded national attention in 1999 when a Blue Mockingbird, an extremely rare stray from Mexico, showed up.

To reach the site from the intersection of Texas Highway 88 and Business US 83, drive south on TX 88 (Texas Street) to Twelfth Boulevard and watch for the entrance on the east. The building housing the headquarters and gift shop is located behind the striking 1927 Spanish Colonial Revival Skaggs House, which was donated to Frontera Audubon in 1992 and which will eventually become a historical museum.

At the rear of the house, a mile of trails wind through fifteen acres of grounds, with planted citrus growing among native trees and shrubs. Small marshy ponds and open areas create diversity in the habitat. Much of it is in fact thicketlike: the kind of dense cover that many flycatchers, vireos, thrushes, thrashers, and warblers seem to enjoy. Such typical Valley birds as Black-bellied Whistling-Duck; Plain Chachalaca; White-winged (spring and summer) and White-tipped doves; Couch's Kingbird; Green Jay; Long-billed Thrasher; and Lesser Goldfinch can be found here, and Green Parakeets and Red-crowned Parrots are often in the vicinity. The Frontera thicket really comes into its own, though, in migration, when it may host a broad array of land birds, from hummers to orioles. It's located just minutes from the Valley Nature Center, and both spots should be visited if you're in the Weslaco area.

Frontera Audubon Society
1101 South Texas Boulevard
Weslaco, TX 78599
(956) 968–3275
www.fronteraaudubonsociety.com
Admission fee.

Valley Nature Center

A delightful oasis in downtown Weslaco, the Valley Nature Center (VNC) will reward a visit on several levels. From the intersection of TX 88 and Business 83, drive west on Business 83 2 blocks, turn south on Borders Street, go 1 block, and turn east into Gibson Park.

Inside the visitor center you'll find guidebooks, field guides, and other local nature information; exhibits on the Rio Grande Valley environment; and birding advice and news of current goings-on. The friendly staff is always eager to help travelers.

In the rear, trails totaling three-quarters of a mile wind among native trees and shrubs, the result of intensive efforts to revegetate the center's 6 acres with species found in the area. Many plants are labeled, making the VNC a good place to visit early on a trip to the Valley. Here you can learn the names of some of the flora you'll be seeing elsewhere as you roam the Rio Grande region.

Buff-bellied Hummingbirds may be easier to see here than anyplace else in the Valley. Plain Chachalacas walk among the trees, while the breeze is filled with the calls and songs of White-tipped Dove; Golden-fronted Woodpecker; Great Kiskadee; Black-crested Titmouse; Long-billed and Curve-billed thrashers; and Lesser Goldfinch. Yellow-crowned Night-Heron and Black-bellied Whistling-Duck have nested on the grounds, and Tropical Kingbird, Clay-colored Robin, and Altamira Oriole have been seen. Often Green Parakeets and Red-crowned Parrots come to roost at dusk—if not here, in adjacent residential areas. During spring migration, of course, this patch of greenery is a great place to visit for transient songbirds.

Extensive plantings of lantana, eupatorium, and other flowering species attract butterflies in both numbers and variety, making the VNC one of the real hot spots in the area. Butterfly watcher or not, you're sure to be distracted by the flutterings of beauties such as Bordered Patch, Zebra Heliconian, Gulf Fritillary, and White Peacock. Watch also, especially in the center's cactus garden, for the endangered Texas tortoise, plodding slowly along on its stumpy legs.

Valley Nature Center
P.O. Box 8125
Weslaco, TX 78599
(956) 969–2475
www.valleynaturecenter.org
Admission fee.

Edinburg Scenic Wetlands

This excellent site was the first of the World Birding Center locations to open officially, with a ribbon-cutting ceremony in March 2003. Located just minutes from US 281, it's certain to become one of the most popular spots in the Rio Grande Valley for nature observation. With six acres of butterfly gardens, it will be a destination for butterfly watchers as well as birders. There's even a small pond dedicated to dragonflies, of special interest to the growing number of people interested in watching and identifying these colorful and carnivorous odonates.

To reach the wetlands, take Texas Highway 107 east from US 281 in Edinburg. Drive 0.7 mile and turn south on Raul Longoria Road. In 0.5 mile turn east at Sprague Street into 155-acre Edinburg Municipal Park. Look for the interpretive center on your left (north), with entrance paths leading through the butterfly garden. Inside are displays on the pothole wetlands that once dotted the Rio Grande Valley as well as information about birds and butterflies, interactive computer programs, and a small bookstore. Staff members can answer questions about this site and birding elsewhere in the region.

Outside, you'll find two twenty-acre lakes (part of the city water-treatment facility), 2 miles of trails, observation platforms, and plenty of waterbirds. The sometimes elusive Green Kingfisher is the official city bird of Edinburg, and, fittingly enough, this diminutive species is seen regularly here. Look also for American White Pelican (fall through spring); Neotropic and Double-crested (winter) cormorants; several species of wading birds including Black-crowned and Yellow-crowned night-herons and nesting Least Bittern; Black-bellied Whistling-Duck; wintering dabbling ducks including Cinnamon Teal; shorebirds including nesting Black-necked Stilt; nesting Gull-billed Tern; an occasional Ringed Kingfisher; and wintering Belted Kingfisher. The mesquite trees around the ponds can be good in migration for various songbirds and year-round for typical Valley species such as Great Kiskadee; Couch's Kingbird; Curve-billed Thrasher; and Olive Sparrow.

The center also offers programs including bird and butterfly walks and identification workshops. Check in advance to see what might be on the schedule during your visit.

Edinburg Scenic Wetlands
714 South Raul Longoria Road
Edinburg, TX 78539
(956) 381–9922
Admission fee.

Salt Lake Tracts

The Lower Rio Grande Valley National Wildlife Refuge owns several tracts of unique wetland habitat north of Texas Highway 186 east of its intersection with US 281, about 18 miles north of Edinburg. At the heart of these tracts are hypersaline (i.e., very salty) lakes, with a long history of exploitation for their mineral content. (That use continues today: Though the U.S. Fish and Wildlife Service owns the land, commercial interests still hold mining rights, extracting brine from the lakes.) The whole area is a closed basin, and the hydrology of the lakes is not fully understood by geologists.

Although the areas are mostly undeveloped and not as easy to access as many sites, they're very popular with local birders for migrant and wintering waterfowl, Sandhill Cranes, and shorebirds as well as "western" birds attracted to the arid, scrubby environment.

From US 281, drive east on TX 186 for 3.6 miles to a small parking area and an information board on the north side of the highway. This is one entrance to La Sal del Rey Tract (LTC 5), named "salt of the king" in the days when the Spanish crown controlled the lakes. An old road leads northeast from here to the lake, which has an average depth of 3 to 4 feet and is about 5 miles in circumference. Many birders prefer to access the lake from entrances along Brushline Road (LTC 6). Continue east on TX 186 for 2.2 miles and turn north on Brushline. Look for trailheads on the west side of the road, beginning in about 1.7 miles. From any of these entrances, expect a walk of a half mile or so through arid brushland to the lake. Ferruginous Pygmy-Owl has been seen in this vicinity.

Thousands of Sandhill Cranes come to roost on the lake at dusk in winter, leaving early in the morning to feed in the surrounding agricultural lands. So, too, do flocks of Snow Geese. Depending on the season, you may also find American White Pelican; cormorants; herons and egrets; Wood Stork (late summer); ducks of several species; and varied shorebirds, gulls, and terns. Look for Snowy and Wilson's plovers; Black-necked Stilt; Long-billed Curlew; Wilson's Phalarope (which can be present during migration in flocks of thousands); Gull-billed Tern; and Black Skimmer, to list only a few.

The arid landscape is also good for raptors, including White-tailed Kite; Harris's and White-tailed hawks; and Crested Caracara. In winter, you could find Say's Phoebe; Vermilion Flycatcher; Lark Bunting; or some western stray such as Sage Thrasher or Green-tailed Towhee, in addition to residents such as Greater Roadrunner; Groove-billed Ani; Cactus Wren; Curve-billed Thrasher; and Pyrrhuloxia.

Return to TX 186 and drive east about 3.8 miles to a dirt road on the north, which may be signed County Road 10. Turn north and drive 1.6 miles to a small parking area on the east, which has an information sign and map. You are now in La Sal Vieja–Teniente Tract (LTC 7) of the national wildlife refuge. Various trails and old roads to the east allow exploration for scrubland birds similar to those at La Sal del Rey. Carrying a compass or GPS unit could be useful here.

You can reach another large salt lake by returning to TX 186, driving east 2 miles, and turning north on County Road 30. (At this writing, though, the road is poorly maintained; it may be impassable at times for cars.) In about 2.7 miles you will reach the lake. There are also several spots along CR 30 from which old roads lead east to the lake.

As times passes, there may well be greatly improved access to all these ecologically fascinating and bird-rich areas. It's best to contact the refuge office in advance for the latest information and advice.

Lower Rio Grande Valley National Wildlife Refuge
Route 2, Box 202A
Alamo, TX 78516
(956) 787–3079
southwest.fws.gov/refuges/texas/lrgv.html

The Upper Valley

Take the statement, "I got Clay-colored Robin at Santa Ana and picked up Hook-billed Kite at Bentsen, but I missed the tyrannulet at Anzalduas." Experienced birders know that's a description of a day (or part of one) spent visiting some of the most famous birding sites in the United States.

Santa Ana National Wildlife Refuge, Bentsen–Rio Grande State Park, and Anzalduas County Park are located within a short drive of each other, and all are must-visit hot spots in the Rio Grande Valley. These and a growing list of birding sites protect invaluable tracts of Valley habitat, from riparian woodland to arid thornscrub. The list of birds sought here ranges from Great Kiskadee (which quickly reaches the "It's just another . . ." category) to regular but sometimes frustratingly elusive species such as Hook-billed Kite and Brown Jay to rarities such as Golden-crowned Warbler and Blue Bunting. There are so many possibilities in the Valley, and so many dedicated local birders and visitors searching, that there's rarely a time when the local hot line lacks something pulse-quickening.

It must be said that, with the exception of the interior trails of a few parks, the Rio Grande Valley is not a pretty place to watch birds. It's a flat land (it's a "valley" only in the sense of being near an important river) of towns, malls, and mile after mile of agricultural fields. But when your first Green Kingfisher pops up in your binocular view, you'll forget about the RV parks and freeways.

The Valley makes a warm escape during winter, as thousands of "winter Texans" demonstrate annually. Generally, spring is the best time to visit, when resident birds are supplemented by migrants heading north. Rare birds can appear anytime, though for humans, the Valley summer can be extremely and unmercifully hot.

This chapter begins with near-mythic Santa Ana, small as national wildlife refuges go but huge in the imagination of birders, and ends at the small town of San Ygnacio, known primarily for a single species, which flits through the dense vegetation along the Rio Grande. In between are Muscovy Ducks, Gray Hawks, Red-billed Pigeons, Audubon's Orioles, and—who knows?—maybe a Yellow-faced Grassquit.

The Upper Valley

83 **35**
83 **44**
281
San Diego
44
Alice
59
16
359
Laredo
85
Hebbronville
San Ygnacio
San Ygnacio
16
Rachal
2
Zapata
83
281
Falcon Reservoir
Falcon State Park
755
Falcon Heights
2098
Salineño
Falcon County Park
Santa Margarita Ranch
Falcon Dam
Roma
Chapeño
Rio Grande City
Edinburg
Salineño
Rio Grande
Yturria and La Puerta Tracts
83
107 **336**
493
La Joya
McAllen
Alamo
Mission
Pharr
Donna
Bentsen–Rio Grande State Park
115
MEXICO
Anzalduas County Park
2
907
Santa Ana NWR
N
0 Miles 20

NOTE: It's an unfortunate fact that this area's proximity to Mexico, just across the often narrow and shallow Rio Grande, makes it attractive to illegal immigrants and drug smugglers. The very places birders frequent—isolated wooded trails, for example—also provide cover for illegal activities. Use common sense and caution when birding, especially near the Rio Grande.

For the current birding scoop, call the Rio Grande Valley bird hot line at (956) 584–2731.

World Birding Center

Under development as this book goes to press, the World Birding Center (WBC) is the most visible indication of the Rio Grande Valley's recognition of the impact of visiting birders on the local economy and environment. Part state park, part habitat-protection program, and part tourism-promotion scheme, the WBC has plans for nine locations from South Padre Island to the small town of Roma, upriver almost to Falcon Dam. Its aim is to "significantly increase the appreciation, understanding, and conservation of birds, wildlife, habitat, and Texas' natural heritage for current and future generations through education, community involvement, and sustainable nature tourism."

WBC headquarters, under construction at this writing, is at Bentsen–Rio Grande State Park, one of the nation's legendary birding hot spots. (See the park listing in this chapter for details.) Two new state parks (called "resource" sites) are planned for Estero Llano Grande, south of Weslaco, and Resaca de la Palma, west of Brownsville. Smaller-scale "gateway" sites are proposed for South Padre Island, Harlingen, Edinburg (a fine facility completed and dedicated in March 2003), McAllen, Hidalgo, and Roma. At all sites, visitors will be able to get advice about birding in the Valley and see exhibits on aspects of the local environments. The theme at the Edinburg wetlands, for example, is the ecology of Valley "pothole" lakes.

Because plans are still tentative in some cases, not all these sites have been included in this book. Some of them could well become excellent birding locations. At Hidalgo and Roma, for instance, adjoining tracts of land owned by the Lower Rio Grande National Wildlife Refuge may be opened to the public with nature trails through riparian woods along the river. Resaca de la Palma has the potential to open nearly 2,000 acres to birders. By contrast, McAllen's site, a mansion set on eight acres of landscaped grounds, will be primarily an information center.

For the future, the best advice is to check with WBC headquarters (due to open in early 2004) for birding possibilities. The Web site is www.world birdingcenter.org, and the telephone number (which could change) is (956) 584–9156.

Santa Ana National Wildlife Refuge

Santa Ana has long been one of the most famous birding destinations in the United States, a legendary spot both for its regularly occurring species and for the rarities that have been seen over the years. Set along the looping course of the Rio Grande, Santa Ana at 2,088 acres is relatively small for a national wildlife refuge. Nonetheless, within its subtropical thorn forest, riparian woodland, and wetlands birders have found almost 400 species—including nearly all the south Texas specialties.

These days Santa Ana has more competition for visiting birders' attention than it once did, which is of course a good thing: the result of more parks and preserves being established and opened to the public in the Valley. Still, it remains one of the most rewarding natural areas in the United States, not just for birders but for all outdoor enthusiasts.

Located just south of U.S. Highway 281, southeast of Pharr (0.4 mile east of Texas Highway 907), the refuge is extremely easy to reach. Once you arrive, your strategy will depend on the time of year and time of day of your visit.

First of all, you'll probably notice people standing quietly among the colorful wildflowers between the parking lot and the visitor center. Santa Ana is also one of the top butterfly-watching sites in the country, and this specially planted garden—with milkweed, lantana, blue mist, sage, dalea, and many other flowers—can swarm with a number of the refuge's astounding 250-plus species. If you enjoy butterflies, it could be quite a while before you even make it past this spot, distracted as you might be by Gulf Fritillaries, Zebra Heliconians, Texan Crescents, and White Peacocks.

The refuge visitor center opens at 8:00 A.M., and inside you'll find books, maps, staff members and volunteers ready to offer advice, and a computerized listing of recent bird sightings. Santa Ana receives intense coverage nearly year-round (the very hot summer is the slowest season), so notable species are often tracked day by day. Look up "Altamira Oriole," for example, and you might be directed to the exact spot where a pair is nesting.

Santa Ana's popularity and the need to protect its natural resources have led to restrictions on private-vehicle access to its 7-mile wildlife drive, now allowed only on weekends in summer. Bicycling and walking are allowed anytime. This means that to reach its more remote sections, such as the Vireo Trail to the Rio Grande, can require a lengthy hike (or a fairly short ride).

One alternative is the interpretive tram tour offered several times a day from Thanksgiving through April. A guide narrates the 1.5-hour ride around the wildlife drive. You can also use the tram simply as transportation to a trail-head and then either walk back to the visitor center or catch a later tram.

The most popular of Santa Ana's 12 miles of hiking trails, though, are easily reached from a trailhead just behind the visitor center. These trails (and non-motorized access to the wildlife drive) open at dawn to accommodate birders eager to enjoy peak early-morning activity. The half-mile A Trail is paved and handicapped-accessible, looping to Willow Lake through a beautiful forest of honey mesquite, cedar elm, Rio Grande ash, Texas ebony, and retama, draped with Spanish moss and ball moss. The 1.6-mile B Trail circles Willow Lake, and the 2-mile C Trail winds around Pintail Lake to the bank of the Rio Grande.

Many of the birds sought after by visitors in south Texas are common or fairly common around Santa Ana. A sampling would include Least Grebe; Black-bellied Whistling-Duck; Harris's and Gray hawks; Plain Chachalaca; Groove-billed Ani; Elf Owl (absent in winter); Buff-bellied Hummingbird; Ringed and Green kingfishers; Golden-fronted and Ladder-backed woodpeckers; Brown-crested Flycatcher (rare in winter); Great Kiskadee; Couch's Kingbird (spring through fall); Green Jay; Black-crested Titmouse; Long-billed and Curve-billed thrashers; Olive Sparrow; and Hooded (rare in winter) and Altamira orioles.

Hook-billed Kite is often present but hard to spot; look for birds soaring in midmorning just above the treetops. Common Pauraque is common, but since individuals are usually spotted by the shine of their eyes in automobile head-lights as they rest on roads after dark, they're not often seen here.

Among the many other rare to accidental birds occasionally seen at the refuge are Masked Duck (in vegetation around the edges of ponds); Zone-tailed Hawk (watch carefully; it can look amazingly like a Turkey Vulture when it soars); Red-billed Pigeon; Northern Beardless-Tyrannulet; Rose-throated Becard; Yellow-green Vireo; Clay-colored Robin; Tropical Parula; White-collared Seedeater; and Blue Bunting.

Especially in the warmer seasons, it's important to get an early start while woodland birding at Santa Ana (as elsewhere in the Valley). Singing and other activity decline rapidly a few hours after sunrise, here in the subtropics. Plus, if it's your first visit, you'll want to be present to hear the dawn chorus of Plain Chachalacas, screaming their name in chanting crescendo.

Try to cover as many habitats as you can during your time in the refuge: the lush forest around Willow Lake; the more open landscape around Pintail Lake; marshy vegetation in shallow areas of the lakes; the more arid thornscrub far-ther south in the refuge, as on the Owl, Highland, and Mesquite trails. Santa Ana is certainly one of those well-frequented birding destinations where it pays to chat with people you meet along the trails. Another party may well have just spotted a species you'd like to see.

From mid-March to mid-April, a hawk watch operates on the levee west of the visitor center. By far the most common raptor counted is Broad-winged Hawk; occasionally several thousand are seen in one day. Turkey Vulture, Mississippi Kite, and Swainson's Hawk are also frequent, and rarities can include Peregrine Falcon or even Swallow-tailed Kite.

Santa Ana National Wildlife Refuge
Route 2, Box 202A
Alamo, TX 78516
(956) 784–7500
southwest.fws.gov/refuges/texas/santana.html
Admission fee.

Casa Santa Ana

Perfectly situated for birders visiting famed Santa Ana National Wildlife Refuge (LTC 59), this nature-oriented lodging is located just off US 281, less than a half mile east of the refuge entrance. In fact, guests can walk to the refuge along the levee road, which leads directly to Santa Ana's tour road and hiking trails. Casa Santa Ana features five rooms with private baths, two in the main house and three in a separate wing. Each has its own outside entrance. The inn is operated "home-stay" style, which means guests maintain their own rooms and fix their own breakfasts with provided supplies. Guests also have access to laundry facilities, a recreation room, and a veranda for post-birding relaxation.

Casa Santa Ana
3239 South Tower Road
Alamo, TX 78516
(956) 783–5540
www.casasantaana.com

Alamo Inn

Located in a historic 1919 building and operated by a knowledgeable local naturalist, the Alamo Inn makes a fine base for birders visiting Santa Ana National Wildlife Refuge (LTC 59) and other mid-Valley locations. Four suites with private baths are on the second floor; breakfast is served in the restaurant downstairs, though room service is available. Each suite is decorated in an individual theme related to Rio Grande Valley history, and all have refrigerators, TVs, and telephones. Facing the downtown park in the city of Alamo, the inn also features a bookshop with an excellent selection of field guides, maps, checklists, and other nature-related merchandise.

Alamo Inn
801 Main Street (Business US 83)
Alamo, TX 78516
(956) 782–9912
www.alamoinnsuites.com

Texas Tropics Nature Festival

One of the most popular and diverse nature festivals in Texas is held each March in McAllen, in the heart of the Rio Grande Valley. Though it covers subjects including butterflies, reptiles, local history, and wildflowers, birds are of course a major focus. Each year, nationally known speakers present programs, and field trips range from the Gulf of Mexico to Falcon Dam. A special treat is canoe and boat trips on the Rio Grande, offering a better-than-usual chance to see birds such as Muscovy Duck and Red-billed Pigeon. You'll also find an extensive marketplace of nature-related products as well as seminars on varied topics. Migration is in full swing in late March in the Valley, adding to the number of potential birds.

McAllen Chamber of Commerce
P.O. Box 790
McAllen, TX 78505
(877) 622–5536
www.mcallenchamber.com/tourism/naturefest/

Anzalduas County Park

Anzalduas ranks with the most popular and productive birding sites in the valley, with a notable list of specialties and rarities to its credit. To reach it, take Texas Highway 1016 south from U.S. Highway 83 in Mission about 3.3 miles; turn south on Texas Highway 494, drive past the prominent mission building on the hill, and turn right at the park entrance road. It's best to visit Anzalduas on a weekday if possible, to avoid the crowds of picnickers, boaters, and others enjoying its recreational facilities.

The entrance road passes through a grassy area where Western Meadowlark often winters with Easterns. Sparrows of many species also winter, and wintering Sprague's Pipit has been found.

Appearances can be deceiving, on several levels, as you pass the park entrance station. At first glance the park seems to be too mowed and managed for good birding. And because the Rio Grande makes a tight loop here, you'll have the somewhat disconcerting feeling of looking north into Mexico (to another park across the river). Anzalduas is also bigger than it looks at first.

Drive or walk the road along the river and around the picnic area, looking and listening for Black-crowned Night-Heron (sometimes in riverside trees); Hook-billed Kite; Gray Hawk (nests here regularly); Common Moorhen; Red-billed Pigeon (rarely seen); Ringed and Green kingfishers; Northern Beardless-Tyrannulet (nests regularly); Brown-crested Flycatcher (spring through fall); Couch's Kingbird; Green Jay; Cliff and Cave swallows (spring through fall, and nesting on the dam); Clay-colored Robin; and Altamira Oriole. Vermilion Flycatcher and Eastern Bluebird are common in winter, at which season a mixed flock of warblers often flits through the trees. Rarities seen at Anzalduas with varying frequency include Zone-tailed Hawk; Rose-throated Becard; and Tropical Parula. Even Greater Pewee has appeared here, among Anzalduas's history of birds cited on the local hot line.

Be sure to drive over the levee to the less-developed section of the park on the other side, where you'll have views of the river below the dam (built to divert river water for agriculture). Cormorants, waders, ducks, Osprey, and shorebirds might be present here. Walking the levee road itself can be a good way to spot birds in the trees on either side.

Located between the legendary birding spots of Santa Ana National Wildlife Refuge (LTC 59) and Bentsen–Rio Grande State Park (LTC 69), Anzalduas County Park is a highly accessible spot that deserves a place on every Valley birder's itinerary.

Anzalduas County Park
www.missionchamber.com/anzalduas.html
(956) 585–5311

Rio Grande Canoe Trips

One of the best ways to see some of the special birds of the lower Rio Grande Valley, including Muscovy Duck, Hook-billed Kite, Red-billed Pigeon, and Ringed and Green kingfishers, is to travel along the river itself. A nonprofit group called the Friends of the Wildlife Corridor, founded primarily to support and assist the Santa Ana and Lower Rio Grande Valley national wildlife refuges, conducts regular canoe trips along stretches of the river. Such a trip is an excellent way to bird while experiencing the Rio Grande environment and supporting conservation efforts. Full- and half-day trips are offered, and both include guides, snacks, drinks, and equipment; the full-day trip also includes lunch. For information on the canoe trips and other group activities, contact:

Friends of the Wildlife Corridor
Route 2, Box 204
Alamo, TX 78516
(956) 783–6117
www.corridorfriends.org
Fee for trips.

Bentsen–Rio Grande State Park and World Birding Center Headquarters

Located on the Rio Grande 5 miles southwest of Mission (from Business US 83, take Texas Highway 2062 south), Bentsen has long held a place among the top dozen (perhaps half-dozen) birding sites in the country. The majority of the regular southern Texas specialties have been seen in this relatively small state park, along with a long list of rare strays. A birding trip to the Valley without at least one visit to Bentsen, with its subtropical woods, thornscrub, and resacas (oxbow lakes), has always been unthinkable.

Major changes are under way at Bentsen as this book goes to press, though—changes brought about because of its selection as the headquarters and showplace of the World Birding Center (see chapter introduction). The plans have been somewhat controversial, but WBC and park officials are confident that in the long term the park environment will be healthier and thus more inviting for both birds and people—even if a little less convenient to visit for the latter.

As you approach the park, you'll see the headquarters for the WBC (under construction at this writing, with completion scheduled for early 2004) on the west side of TX 2062 just outside the Rio Grande levee, beyond which lies the main park. There are plans to revegetate the area surrounding the center (former agricultural land) to create habitat for birds and butterflies. Inside the headquarters, you'll find exhibits, maps, nature guidebooks and checklists, advice on birding the entire Valley, and news of the latest sightings.

In the biggest change to the park, private vehicles will no longer be allowed into Bentsen. Instead, trams will shuttle visitors around the park roads. Officials have promised an early-morning tram for birders who wish to enter at dawn, when birds are most active. There are also plans to allow entry at night for owling and searching for Common Pauraque. Small golf-cart–like vehicles may also be available, and entry on foot or by bicycle will be permitted anytime the park is open.

For some, birding at Bentsen has been a social event: Visitors parked their RVs, put out feeders, posted sightings boards, and served as informal birding guides. Many people saw their first Clay-colored Robin or Blue Bunting in the Bentsen camping area. Recreational vehicles are now banned from the park, and the only camping allowed will be primitive tent camping, with overnighters carrying in all their equipment on foot. (RVing will be available at a private development near the park.) There are plans, though, to continue feeding birds (in an "environmentally sound manner and primarily for educational purposes") and to create viewing areas with hummingbird feeders and watering sites. In addition, the park will build a hawk-watch tower and birding walkways.

At the same time, state park officials will be trying to alter and improve water flow through the park, which without question has been suffering in recent years from drought. Areas that once were lush riparian vegetation of elm, ash, ebony, and hackberry have seen the death of trees and shrubs and the invasion of arid-land species. Changing visitation patterns in the park and eliminating most camping is said to be helpful to this habitat-improvement process.

All in all, Bentsen will continue to be just as birdy a spot, and quite possibly birdier. It will be less easy to travel around the park, freely moving from one site to another, especially for persons with limited mobility who use their vehicles as bases from which to bird.

And speaking of birds: The list of noteworthy possibilities at Bentsen is essentially the list of Rio Grande Valley specialties, with few exceptions. As one illustration, in 2003 visitors could stand in one spot and see nesting Gray Hawk, Elf Owl, and Northern Beardless-Tyrannulet. Bentsen has always been one of the best spots to look for Hook-billed Kite; Red-billed Pigeon; and Tropical Parula. Species such as Plain Chachalaca; White-winged (spring through fall) and White-tipped doves; Golden-fronted and Ladder-backed woodpeckers; Brown-crested Flycatcher (spring through fall); Couch's Kingbird; Green Jay; Black-crested Titmouse; Long-billed Thrasher; Olive Sparrow; and Altamira Oriole are common. The scarce and sporadic White-collared Seedeater has appeared at Bentsen recently, perhaps part of an expansion in range from its regular spots farther up the Rio Grande. Both Ringed and Green kingfishers show up frequently at park resacas. Extreme rarities found at Bentsen have included Roadside Hawk; Collared Forest-Falcon; Masked Tityra; and Crimson-collared Grosbeak—all strays from Mexico and certainly not to be expected.

The U.S. Fish and Wildlife Service owns more than 1,700 acres adjacent to Bentsen as part of the Lower Rio Grande Valley National Wildlife Refuge (a parcel not open at this writing), and in the future park trails will connect with refuge trails to offer access to nearly 2,500 acres of habitat. It's not possible to predict exactly how birding opportunities will change in years to come. As always, the best advice is to talk to park officials and naturalists about spots to visit and the most productive trails to walk at the time of your visit. There's little question, though, that Bentsen will continue as one of the nation's best and most famous birding destinations.

Bentsen–Rio Grande State Park
P.O. Box 988
Mission, TX 78573
(956) 585–1107
www.tpwd.state.tx.us/park/bentsen
Admission fee.

World Birding Center
(956) 584–9156
www.worldbirdingcenter.org

Texas Butterfly Festival

More and more birders and other nature enthusiasts are becoming interested in butterflies, thanks in part to new identification guides and the increasing availability of close-focus binoculars. In recognition of this trend—and of the fact that the Rio Grande Valley is the best place in the United States to see a wide variety of species—the Valley town of Mission celebrates the Texas Butterfly Festival each October (the best month for butterfly watching in the region). Field trips to parks and gardens allow looks at common butterflies such as Large Orange Sulphur, Zebra Heliconian, and White Peacock, and a chance at specialties such as Red-bordered Pixie, Mexican Bluewing, and Guava Skipper. Speakers present programs, identification workshops, and photography classes.

Texas Butterfly Festival
220 East Ninth Street
Mission, TX 78572
(800) 580–2700
www.texasbutterfly.com

Yturria and La Puerta Tracts

These disjunct areas of the Lower Rio Grande Valley National Wildlife Refuge are located directly on US 83 between La Joya and Rio Grande City. Both are undeveloped except for some old roads allowing foot access, both are narrow tracts of land stretching north for a couple of miles from the highway, and both, with their upland thornscrub habitat, are known as good places to see birds associated with more arid country farther west. Both provide little shade, and visits on sunny days can be very hot indeed. (Arrive at dawn if possible.) Nonetheless, they offer good birding and a different experience from exploring sites along the Rio Grande. Yturria's vegetation is a little denser than La Puerta's, and it's probably the place to visit if you have time for only one of these tracts. Contact the refuge office for information and maps in advance of a visit.

The entrance to Yturria Tract (LTC 72) is located on the north side of US 83 about 3.1 miles west of the intersection with Texas Highway 2221 at La Joya. Look for a small parking spot and an informational kiosk. Then simply walk in, following old roads for as far as you wish. The layout of the tract makes it pretty hard to lose your bearings, but it never hurts to carry a compass and keep up with your location.

Some of the more-or-less "western" birds to look for here include Scaled Quail; Greater Roadrunner; Vermilion (winter) and Ash-throated (spring and summer) flycatchers; Bell's Vireo (spring through fall; scarce); Verdin; Cactus Wren; Black-tailed Gnatcatcher (scarce, at the edge of its range here); Cassin's and Black-throated sparrows; Pyrrhuloxia; Varied Bunting (spring through fall); and Bullock's Oriole (spring through fall). Other species you might find include White-tailed Kite; Harris's Hawk; Crested Caracara; Northern Bobwhite; Yellow-billed Cuckoo (spring through fall); Groove-billed Ani; Lesser Nighthawk (spring through fall); Ladder-backed Woodpecker; Brown-crested and Scissor-tailed flycatchers (both spring through fall); White-eyed Vireo; Bewick's Wren; Olive and Lark sparrows; and Painted Bunting.

To reach La Puerta Tract (LTC 74), drive west on US 83 about 18 miles to the outskirts of Rio Grande City. Near the spot where the divided highway ends, look on the north side of the road for a small parking lot, a kiosk, and a gate in the fence. Here again, an old road runs north from the highway through scrub vegetation. Take plenty of water when you leave your car, and watch for snakes.

Lower Rio Grande Valley National Wildlife Refuge
Route 2, Box 202A
Alamo, TX 78516
(956) 787–3079
southwest.fws.gov/refuges/texas/lrgv.html

Santa Margarita Ranch

Santa Margarita Ranch is a large, privately owned tract of mesquite and prickly pear brush and riparian vegetation along the Rio Grande upstream from Roma, and it is a longtime favorite Valley birding location. Reaching it and exploring it can be just slightly more adventurous than is the case at most other local sites, but a visit here is often a highly rewarding experience. This is not a spot for people who have difficulty walking, since it involves a moderate hike over uneven dirt roads. The owners require birders to pay a fee to enter their property, and it's money well spent.

From the old-town section of Roma, travel north on US 83 for 6.9 miles to a paved road on the west (old US 83). Take this road 0.7 mile to a gravel road on the left; follow it 0.7 miles to a T junction. Turn right, drive 0.4 mile, turn left, and drive to the houses. Stop at the blue house to pay (honk to let someone know you're here), and then continue a short distance to a parking area at a metal gate. Walk in past the gate, and where the main road turns left, continue on a minor track straight ahead. Santa Margarita is best birded early in the morning. Not only are birds singing more, but the walk can be quite hot later in the day, even in spring.

As you walk through the mesquite scrub, look and listen for Plain Chachalaca; Scaled Quail; White-winged Dove (spring through fall); Common Ground-Dove; Greater Roadrunner; Lesser Nighthawk (spring through fall); Ladder-backed Woodpecker; Couch's Kingbird (rare in winter); Chihuahuan Raven; Black-crested Titmouse; Verdin; Bewick's Wren; Curve-billed Thrasher; Olive and Black-throated sparrows; and Pyrrhuloxia. There are tracks (cattle paths) you can explore to the sides, but watch for snakes and spiny vegetation.

You will reach another dirt road paralleling the Rio Grande, bordered by a fence. The lushest woodland, with some of the area's best birds, is between this fence and the river. Because the fence excludes grazing cattle, the undergrowth is very thick, and walking through it can be difficult. It's here, however, and on the riverbank, that you have the best chance for species such as Muscovy and Wood ducks; "Mexican"-type Mallard; Gray Hawk; Red-billed Pigeon (Santa Margarita is an excellent spot for this elusive species); White-tipped Dove; Groove-billed Ani (regular here); Common Pauraque; Ringed and Green king-fishers; Brown-crested Flycatcher (spring through fall); Green and Brown (once regular here, now rare) jays; Clay-colored Robin; Long-billed Thrasher; and Altamira and Audubon's orioles.

Many rarities have appeared at Santa Margarita over the years, including Sulphur-bellied Flycatcher, which once nested here. Whether you spot a "hot line" bird or not, a spring morning at the ranch will probably bring several notable sightings, along with the fun of feeling that you're off the beaten path of nature centers, park trails, and observation platforms.

Salineño

Though this spot on the Rio Grande is quite limited in area, it has been one of the traditional sites from which birders scan the river in hopes of finding some of its sought-after specialties. To reach it, look for the Salineño sign on US 83 about 10.2 miles north of Roma or 4.1 miles south of Texas Highway 2098. Turn west here (River Road) and drive to the small community. Keep right at the cemetery, take the unpaved road to the right of the church, and continue to the riverbank.

With lots of luck, you could look out over the Rio Grande as a Ringed or Green kingfisher flies by, or as a Muscovy Duck, Hook-billed Kite, or Red-billed Pigeon appears. More likely are cormorants, various wintering ducks, Osprey (fall through spring), or Bank Swallow (nests in nearby river banks).

On the downstream side of the road is a small fenced tract of land owned by the Lower Rio Grande Valley National Wildlife Refuge. Once an RV park, it was known for bird feeders where jays, orioles, and other species appeared; the elusive Brown Jay was regular. At this writing there are still resident birders who maintain feeders, and there are plans for a bird observatory of some sort. Whatever transpires, this wooded area will be worth visiting for White-tipped Dove (spring through fall); Brown-crested Flycatcher (spring through fall); Green Jay; Long-billed Thrasher; and Audubon's Oriole (scarce), among other birds. Quite a few rarities have appeared here over the years, and such special birds as Groove-billed Ani, Brown Jay, and Clay-colored Robin could appear anytime.

You can also follow an informal trail through the hackberries on the river side of the fence for a short distance downstream.

Lower Rio Grande Valley National Wildlife Refuge
Route 2, Box 202A
Alamo, TX 78516
(956) 787–3079
southwest.fws.gov/refuges/texas/lrgv.html

Chapeño

Though the situation is improving as this book is being written, there are still relatively few places that provide good public access to the Rio Grande between Falcon Dam (LTC 83) and the Gulf of Mexico. As a result, this little spot just below the dam has long been popular with birders visiting the area of the dam and Falcon State Park (LTC 84).

From US 83 about 14 miles west of Roma, take TX 2098 west for 2.8 miles and turn south. (Look for a sign advertising El Rio RV Park opposite a small church.) Continue on this side road for 2.7 miles to the RV park. The park charges a fee for birders to access its eight-and-a-half acres along the Rio Grande, and the birds are usually well worth the price of admission. In recent years this spot has been the most reliable place in the United States to see Brown Jay. The park owners feed the jays twice each morning, and hundreds of people have seen this elusive species here for the first time.

Along the river, look for such birds as Pied-billed Grebe; various waders; Neotropic Cormorant; Muscovy Duck (rare); Osprey (fall through spring); and Ringed and Green kingfishers (Chapeño is one of the most reliable spots in the area for the Green). In trees and shrubs, look for Harris's Hawk; Plain Chachalaca; White-winged (summer), Inca, and White-tipped doves; Golden-fronted Woodpecker; Green Jay; Black-crested Titmouse; Verdin; Long-billed Thrasher; Olive Sparrow; Painted Bunting; Bronzed Cowbird; and Altamira and Audubon's orioles. Among the rarities sometimes spotted here are Hook-billed Kite; Gray and Zone-tailed hawks; Red-billed Pigeon; and Ferruginous Pygmy-Owl. Great Horned Owl has nested regularly in the RV park.

You can also continue a short distance past the RV park entrance and exit roads and turn right to reach the Rio Grande at the end of a short dirt road. Informal trails lead downstream to various viewpoints over the river. Access isn't as good here as at the RV park, but the site is still worth checking.

Falcon County Park and Falcon Dam

At this writing, access to the Falcon Dam spillway has been restricted because of security concerns. In the future birders may again be able to explore this area.

Falcon Dam (LTC 83) and nearby Falcon County Park (LTC 82) are usually visited by birders also stopping at Chapeño (LTC 81) and Falcon State Park (LTC 84), just a few miles away. To reach the dam take TX 2098 west from US 83 about 14 miles northwest of Roma. At the highway intersection just past the town of Falcon Heights (3.3 miles from US 83), turn left on Spur TX 2098.

On your immediate right here is Falcon County Park, worth visiting for some of the same "western" birds as those at Falcon State Park, including Scaled Quail; Greater Roadrunner; Vermilion Flycatcher (winter); Verdin; Cactus Wren; Black-tailed Gnatcatcher (scarce); Pyrrhuloxia; and Black-throated Sparrow. Take time to check areas of scrubby mesquite woods away from the highway.

Continue west toward Falcon Dam on Spur TX 2098. As you approach the dam, watch for a secondary paved road slanting to the left, running below the grassy levee. (The main road crosses the dam into Mexico.) The expanse of lawnlike grass here may have Sprague's Pipit in winter. The secondary road ends at a parking area overlooking the spillway, from which you can scan for waterbirds in and around the Rio Grande below. This is a good spot for Ringed Kingfisher.

An old road leads from a locked gate down the hill paralleling the river into nice riparian woodland. In years past, walking this road was a popular way to look for species such as Red-billed Pigeon; Ferruginous Pygmy-Owl (very scarce recently); and Brown Jay. However, smugglers and other unsavory types sometimes also frequent this area, and many birders now prefer to look for these species elsewhere. While the odds of any sort of trouble are slim, this is a spot about which it might be best to ask local birders for the current situation. Traveling in a small group would help assure safety in visiting this area, which despite lessened visitation has lost none of its birding potential.

Falcon Dam
(956) 848–5221 or (956) 849–1678

Falcon State Park

Situated on the shore of sprawling Falcon Reservoir, this 572-acre state park is one of the few places for tent camping in the lower Rio Grande Valley. (It has spaces for RVs as well.) Its scrub woodland of mesquite, Texas ebony, blackbrush acacia, huisache, and Texas olive, combined with grassland dotted with prickly pear, hosts many Valley specialties. If you've traveled here from the east, you'll notice that this region has a more western feeling than sites farther downstream, a circumstance reflected in the birdlife, too. You may well see a Greater Roadrunner trotting along the roadside as you enter, and you could hear a Cactus Wren singing as you get out of your car.

Reach the park by turning west from US 83 on TX 2098 about 14 miles northwest of Roma. Continue past the small community of Falcon Heights to Park Road 46 and the park entrance. Ask at the entrance station for a park bird list.

Drive or walk the park roads or explore the 3 miles of hiking trails that make a loop around the developed campground. (One mile of the trail is a self-guided nature walk.) As you do, look for Harris's Hawk; Scaled Quail; Inca Dove; Common Ground-Dove; Lesser Nighthawk (spring through fall); Golden-fronted and Ladder-backed woodpeckers; Brown-crested Flycatcher (spring though fall); Chihuahuan Raven; Verdin; Black-tailed Gnatcatcher (rare); Bewick's Wren; Long-billed and Curve-billed thrashers; Pyrrhuloxia; Varied (rare) and Painted buntings (both spring through fall); Cassin's, Lark, and Black-throated sparrows; and Bronzed Cowbird.

There may be various birds frequenting the lake, including American White Pelican; Double-crested (winter) and Neotropic cormorants; ducks; and Osprey (fall through spring). Somewhat surprisingly, Gull-billed Tern nests in the vicinity, so watch for this species as well. The presence of birds and the variety of species are influenced by the level of the reservoir, which can vary greatly.

The park is located only a few minutes from both Chapeño (LTC 81) and Falcon Dam (LTC 83).

Falcon State Park
P.O. Box 2
Falcon Heights, TX 78545
(956) 848–5327
www.tpwd.state.tx.us/park/falcon
Admission fee.

San Ygnacio

For many years, birders visiting the Lower Rio Grande Valley have made the drive upriver to this small town, about 55 miles northwest of Roma, to look for one special bird: White-collared Seedeater, a tiny sparrowlike species that's common in Mexico and Central America but that appears sporadically in an extremely limited range north of the U.S. border. The seedeater is almost always found in dense vegetation near the Rio Grande, and San Ygnacio has long been the most reliable spot.

From US 83 in the center of San Ygnacio, take Washington Street west about 7 blocks to its end at Trevino Street. Look for a path down to the Rio Grande marked with signs and birding notes. The property along the river is privately owned, and a fee is required to enter. The owner has been using the money in part to stock feeders and watering stations and create butterfly gardens in the area.

Some luck is needed to find a seedeater; early morning and late afternoon are usually best. In spring, males sometimes perch atop a tall reed and sing their sweet whistled song, but often the birds skulk in the thick vegetation. Be patient and enjoy looking for other birds including Red-billed Pigeon (rare), Green Kingfisher, Great Kiskadee, Green Jay, and other typical Valley species. If the owner is present (he operates an RV park downriver a short distance), he can offer advice.

Seedeaters are sometimes found at the small wetland behind the public library in Zapata, 14 miles south of San Ygnacio. The Valley hot line may have current information about the status of the species. Recently seedeaters have been seen at Santa Ana National Wildlife Refuge (LTC 59) and Bentsen–Rio Grande Valley State Park (LTC 69), and there is some thought that they may be expanding their range.

Further Reading

There are many birding sites in the Texas Gulf Coast region and nearby that are not part of the Great Texas Coastal Birding Trail. For detailed information on other birding opportunities in Texas, consult the following:

A Birder's Guide to the Rio Grande Valley, by Mark W. Lockwood, William B. McKinney, James N. Paton, and Barry R. Zimmer (American Birding Association, 1999).

A Birder's Guide to the Texas Coast, by Harold R. Holt (American Birding Association, 1993).

Birding Texas, by Roland H. Wauer and Mark A. Elwonger (Falcon Publishing, 1998).

About the Author

Author Mel White specializes in nature and travel writing and is contributing editor for *National Geographic Traveler* and *Living Bird* magazines. In addition to winning the 2002 Lowell Thomas Award for best environmental journalism article, he authored *National Geographic Guide to Birdwatching Sites* and *A Birder's Guide to Arkansas*, among other titles. Likes Bartok, cornbread, Shiraz, the Rockies, and old foreign movies.

Index